GREAT CONVERSIONS

FREDERICK S. LEAHY

AMBASSADOR

BELFAST ◆ **GREENVILLE**
NORTHERN IRELAND SOUTH CAROLINA

GREAT CONVERSIONS
First published 1983
Revised and enlarged edition 1998
Copyright © 1998 Frederick S. Leahy

ISBN 1 84030 031 0

Ambassador Publications
a division of
Ambassador Productions Ltd.
Providence House
16 Hillview Avenue,
Belfast, BT5 6JR
Northern Ireland

Emerald House
1 Chick Springs Road, Suite 203
Greenville,
South Carolina 29609, USA

www.emeraldhouse.com

LIST OF CONTENTS

❖❖❖

INTRODUCTION

❖

Much of the material in this book first appeared as a series of articles in "The Covenanter Witness" (1981-82), the magazine of the Reformed Presbyterian Church. In each case the plan was to tell something of the person's background and way of life before conversion, what is known of the conversion itself, and the long-term results of the conversion. First published in 1983 **Great Conversions** has now been revised and enlarged.

It is doubtful if any Christian can fully appreciate the wonder of conversion. Certainly many, if not most Christians need to give much more thought to this experience of God's sovereign grace and the spiritual renewal wrought by the Holy Spirit. To have one's sins forgiven, to be delivered from the power of Satan and the dominion of sin, to become a child of God, a member of the body of Christ, to be indwelt and sealed by the Holy Spirit to the day of complete redemption of body and soul, to have a vital and loving fellowship with the Lord Jesus Christ and to be assured of dwelling with Him and all the redeemed in Heaven and in this life walking in holiness (and where there is no holiness there has been no conversion) - this is a spiritual reality so stupendous as to transcend the capacity of human understanding. The radical nature and the sheer magnificence of the 'new birth', or regeneration, which issues in a conscious conversion marked by true repentance and saving faith, should constantly fill our hearts with wonder, joy, praise and gratitude. What more could a redeemed sinner want or need save Heaven itself? The 'new birth' is a miracle of God's grace and power and it is imposs- ible to exaggerate its spiritual sufficiency. Doubtless we shall see things more clearly when with the ransomed hosts before the Throne we join in the refrain, "Worthy is the Lamb that was slain ..."

As the Table of Contents shows, these examples of conversion have been selected from a wide diversity of denominational backgrounds and most of the names listed are known to Christians throughout the world.

Historically, the reader begins with the Church Father, Augustine, and concludes with conversions of more modern times.

I have researched the articles to the best of my ability, and am satisfied that they are a reasonably accurate account of these conversions. The first article begins with a brief statement of the Reformed doctrine of conversion, stressing again its importance, and in the remaining chapters the theology is more implicit than explicit. Throughout, the aim has been to tell each story as it happened and as objectively as possible. My interest has never been merely academic. I have often been deeply moved by these accounts and I trust that they will be used by God to speak to others of the importance and necessity of conversion. Above all, it is my prayer that in recalling these conversions and reminding others of them the Name of God may be glorified.

In the original articles I was indebted to Rev. W. E. Leach, M.A., who read the chapter on Samuel Bill; to Rev. J. C. Wright who supplied valuable information (never previously published) about his martyred brother, Fred, and also to Lt. Col. H. Wright who provided confirmation of some of the details. Now I am further indebted to Pastor N. C. Barr of Portadown for the loan of several authoritative works on the life and labours of William Carey, including the classic biography by his great grandson, Rev. S. Pearce Carey; to Rev. Professor Adam Loughridge and Mr. S. W. Murray for information on the conversion of W. P. Nicholson.

"Except ye be converted, and become as little children, ye shall not enter into the kingdom of heaven." (Matthew 18:3)

Prof. F. S. Leahy M. Th.
Reformed Theological College
Belfast

"I AM SO GRATEFUL HE LED ME TO
HIMSELF WHEN I WAS YOUNG SO THAT I
COULD HAVE THIS LONG EARTHLY WALK
WITH HIM. I RECOMMEND HIM AS A
PEERLESS MASTER."

❖❖❖

ISOBEL KUHN

AUGUSTINE

All conversions are great in that they result from God's grace and the quickening power of His Holy Spirit. So when we speak of "great conversions", we refer to conversions of men and women who were used mightily by God in His service and kingdom.

Conversion is the overflow into the conscious life of that radical change effected by the Holy Spirit in regeneration and as a result the one-time indifferent or rebellious sinner repents and seeks mercy from the hand of Christ. Conversion is also a covenant-response, a moment when the whole person responds by God's grace in loving loyalty to God's covenant of grace in Jesus Christ. In conversion the renewed person pledges loving loyalty and undivided allegiance to Christ as the Saviour and King, and that is a covenant-response. It is intrinsic in the experience we call conversion. In Isaiah 56:6, "foreigners" who join themselves to the Lord are said to "embrace" or "hold fast" to His covenant. John Calvin applies this to believers today: "Here he describes the zeal and steadfastness of those who submit themselves to God and cleave to His word; and therefore, if we are joined to God by a covenant, we ought to hold by it constantly, and adhere firmly to sound doctrine, so that it may not be possible to withdraw or separate us from Him in any manner."

Any theology which fails to emphasise the absolute essentiality and the glory of conversion, or which makes it merely preparatory for some greater blessing to be experienced in this life, is unscriptural and misleading.

We begin this series of brief studies of outstanding conversions with the story of how Augustine found forgiveness and peace. Augustine was born at Tagaste, North Africa, in 354, the son of a pagan father and a Christian mother. He studied rhetoric with a view to becoming a lawyer, but he soon decided to devote himself exclusively to literary pursuits. His conversion took place in 386. However there is some evidence to suggest that his dramatic conversion was the culmination of a gradual process which God produced in his life since childhood and which, on certain occasions, came to the surface of his conscious life. The influence of a godly mother, Monica, and the teaching received in his youth never really deserted him and repeatedly emerged to confront his wayward and dissolute life. When he read Cicero's *Hortensius* in 373, his prayers were awakened and he yearned to "return" to God (Confessions, III. chp. 4). He was, at that time, "on fire to leave earthly things behind and fly back" to God. There was but one obstacle: "the name of Christ was not there: for this name, Lord, this name of my Saviour, your Son, had been with my mother's milk drunk in devoutly by my tender heart, where it remained deeply treasured" (Confessions, III. chp. 4). Later he writes, "For want of truth I toiled and I tossed, for I was seeking for you, my God."

In 385, in Milan, Augustine came under the influence of Ambrose who was, as he put it, "healthily teaching salvation." He adds, "But salvation is far from sinners of the kind that I was then. Yet, though I did not realise it, I was drawing gradually nearer." (Confessions IV chp. 13). In those days he experienced much restlessness: "I was storm tossed and you held the tiller" (Confessions VI chp. 5). Again, "I was swept away to you by your beauty, and then I was torn away from you by my own weight and fell back groaning toward these lower things" (Confessions VII chp. 17).

In view of this recurring struggles in Augustine's life - and many more examples of that conflict could be given - in view of his inability to live comfortably in sin or to cease thinking about God and evil (and even his early obsession with occultism) it would seem wise to see his conversion as the *end* of a long process in which God had been dealing with him and drawing him slowly to Himself: in those storm tossed years God "held the tiller".

Finally the great and blessed crisis came. In early August 386 Augustine abandoned his teaching career and his proposed marriage and with some friends, Alypius and Nebridius, returned to an estate near Milan, there to live a life of contemplation. One day on hearing how some men had been moved to devote themselves to the service of God, Augustine's whole life of sin suddenly confronted him. Closely followed by Alypius, he rushed into the garden crying, "What is the matter with us? ... the uninstructed start up and take heaven and we with all our learning but so little heart - see where we wallow in flesh and blood!" He kept saying , "Let it be done now!" But nothing happened. His old lusts and vanities seemed to mock his aching heart. He flung himself under a fig tree and wept bitterly, crying out to God, "How long, how long, tomorrow and tomorrow? Why not now? Why should there not be at this hour an end to my baseness?" (Confessions VIII chp. 12). Then from a neighbouring house he heard a child's voice repeat the words, "Tolle, lege," - "Take and read!" He hastened back to the bench where Alypius was sitting and seized the copy of the Pauline Epistles which he had left there. His eyes fell on the open page and this is what he read, " ...not in rioting and drunkenness, not in chambering and watonness, not in strife and envying: but put ye on the Lord Jesus Christ, and make not provision for the flesh, to fulfil the lusts thereof." (Romans 13: 13,14). It was the answer to his prayer. The fight was over. The battle was won. (Confessions VIII chp. 12). Immediately he told Alypius, keeping his finger in the book to mark the place. He was calm in mind. All passion was spent. Alypius looked at the page and saw what Augustine had missed: "Him that is weak in the faith receive ye." (Romans 14: 1), and he applied this to himself. So together they went and told Monica who was overwhelmed with joy and blessed God. Over the years she had prayed for her wayward son with tears. Now her prayers were answered and her heart's wish was granted.

Thus God in His grace confronted Augustine as dramatically as He did Paul or Luther. This "end" to a long struggle was also the beginning of a life of teaching and service which was to lay the foundations of Western theology and in some senses Western civilisation. We owe an incalculable debt to the African Church Father who experienced our human life and sin and also God's saving grace some 15 centuries before we did. Augustine's whole experience is summed up in words from the opening prayer of his Confessions - "our hearts are restless until they can find peace in You."

MARTIN LUTHER

---◆---

I t was on the 10th November, 1483, in the mining town of Eisleben in Germany, that Margaret, the wife of Hans Luther, gave birth to a son to be called Martin. Martin was brought up in poverty, his father working at different times as a woodcutter, miner and smelter of copper ore. His home life was significant in that both parents were pious, teaching their children the Ten Commandments, the Creed and the Lord's Prayer. Principal T. M. Lindsay makes the point that this teaching which Luther received as a child was "the seed of his theology," for he was taught that pardon comes from the free grace of God. Lindsay states that "the truth which Luther afterward preached to all men he learned in the home circle .. adding nothing essential."

Luther was brought up strictly and at times severely, both at home and at school. Later in life he considered that his upbringing had been too harsh. "It was necessary to punish," he said, "but the apple should be placed beside the rod." Chastisement and fear were the chief incentives to study in Luther's day it is little wonder that every time he heard his teachers speak of Jesus Christ he turned pale, for the Saviour had been presented to him only as an offended Judge. His religion was marked by servile fear.

Hans Luther wished to make his son a scholar and sent him to the Franciscan school at Magdeburg at the age of 14. In great poverty, often begging for the money necessary for his studies and livelihood, he excelled as a student. Merle D'Aubigne writes, "The strength of his understanding, the liveliness of his imagination, the excellence of his memory, soon carried him beyond all his schoolfellows." At 18, in 1501, he was sent to the university of Erfurt. At this stage Luther was having serious thoughts about God and he spent much time in prayer and other religious exercises. "To pray well," he used to say, "is the better half of study."

The young student spent most of his spare time in the university library. Books were rare in those days and were regarded as treasures. Luther had been two years in Erfurt when one volume in particular attracted his attention: it was a Bible. Until then he had thought that the selections from the Gospels and Epistles read at the services comprised the whole Word of God. Now he saw many books of which he had never even heard! With eagerness and intense emotion he read the Bible. That same year he received his bachelor's degree and some years later, in 1505, he was admitted master of arts and doctor of philosophy. Now Luther was ready to apply himself to the study of Law as his father wished him to do. However the hunger of his heart remained unsatisfied and it was in the midst of a terrible thunderstorm that Luther, filled with fear, fell to his knees and vowed that if the Lord should deliver him from this danger he would abandon the world and devote himself entirely to God's service.

On 17th August, 1505, Luther, aged 21, in the darkness of night, knocked on the gate of the Augustinian convent in Erfurt. He was determined to find peace with God. The monks received this distinguished scholar with joy and then proceeded to humble him by treating him harshly and giving him the most menial tasks to perform. Again he turned to the Scriptures, this time in their original languages. At the same time he sought to mortify the flesh by fastings and scourgings. "Never," writes D'Aubigne, "did the Romish church possess a more pious monk." Later in life Luther wrote: "If ever a monk could obtain heaven by his monkish works, I should certainly have been entitled to it." But Luther's "monkish works" brought him no peace.

At this time the vicar-general of the Augustines was John Staupitz, who after a long struggle had himself found peace through faith in Christ. Staupitz on a visit to Erfurt was quick to notice Luther. Observing that the young monk was dejected and scarcely touching his food, Staupitz engaged him in conversation. Luther quickly unburdened his heart, "Look at the wounds of Jesus Christ," urged Staupitz, "to the blood that He has shed for you. Instead of torturing yourself on account of your sins, throw yourself into the Redeemer's arms. Trust in Him - in the righteousness of His life - in the atonement of His death." But Luther held back. One day an aged monk reminded him of the words of the Apostle's Creed: "I believe in the forgiveness of sins." Luther agreed. "Ah!" said the monk, "you must believe not only in the forgiveness of David's and Peter's sins, for even the devils believe. It is God's command that we believe our own sins are forgiven us ... The testimony of the Holy Spirit is this: Thy sins are forgiven thee." It was at that moment that the light dawned in Luther's soul and he found peace. The word of grace had been spoken and he believed it. He did not yet see all the implications and consequences of this belief, but the great change had taken place. He renounced all human merit and resigned himself unreservedly to the grace of God in Jesus Christ. Later his faith was confirmed and strengthened by his study of Paul's Epistle to the Romans, particularly Paul's quotation of the words of Habakkuk, "The just shall live by faith." "Straightway," he wrote, "I felt as if I were born anew. It was as if I had found the door of Paradise thrown wide open. Now I saw the Scriptures altogether in a new light ... The expression, 'the righteousness of God,' which I so much hated before now became dear and precious - my darling and comforting word." The words of Staupitz came back to him, that the righteousness of God for all who trust in Christ is on the sinner's side and not against him."

Years later Luther declared: "I hated Paul with all my heart when I read that the righteousness of God is revealed in the Gospel (Romans 1:16,17). Only afterward, when I saw the words that follow - namely, that it is written that the righteous shall live through faith ... was I cheered." As Philip Schaff puts it, "He had trembled like a slave, now he rejoiced as a son in his father's house." Luther had found the answer to the all-important question, "What must I do to be saved?" The answer was clear, "Believe on the Lord Jesus Christ, and thou shalt be saved, and thy house." From that day forth his watchword was *sola fide* - **by faith alone**.

HUGH LATIMER

❖

Hugh Latimer was born about 1485 at Thurcaston in Leicestershire. His father tilled a small farm, keeping one hundred sheep and some thirty cows. He did his best for his children, seeing that his daughters were well married and sending his son, Hugh, to Cambridge at the age of fourteen. In 1509 Hugh was elected a Fellow of Clare Hall.

Latimer's birthplace was just twelve miles from Lutterworth, where 140 years earlier John Wycliffe had encouraged the reading of the Scriptures by preparing an English translation from the Latin Vulgate. Wycliffe's followers, the Lollards, preached from handwritten copies of this translation, for printing had not yet been introduced to England, and so the "heresy" spread throughout the land! Latimer's father had shielded him from the teaching of the Lollards and until the age of thirty he was strongly Roman Catholic in his beliefs. Later he declared in one of his sermons, "I was as obstinate a Papist as any was in England, insomuch that when I should be made bachelor of divinity, my whole oration went against Philip Melanchthon and his opinions." There was applause as Latimer concluded his discourse. The dons were pleased. Here was a man, they felt, who could confound the German heretics and save the Church in England. Latimer was so appalled by the teaching of the Reformers that he declared that the end of the world must be approaching!

One man who listened to Latimer's onslaught against Melanchthon was a student named Thomas Bilney, a contemporary of Latimer's at Cambridge. Bilney had studied the Scriptures and found salvation in Christ alone through faith. He saw in Latimer another Saul of Tarsus, full of "zeal for God, but not enlightened." As he watched and listened, Bilney prayed for wisdom. Shortly afterwards he knocked on Latimer's door. Latimer was amazed when Bilney asked him to hear his confession. So the heretic wanted to confess! Latimer was triumphant, thinking that his sermon had converted Bilney. The confession to which he listened was not what he had expected. Bilney recounted his spiritual pilgrimage and told of his vain search for peace through penance and masses and suchlike and how, after reading Erasmus's New Testament, he had found peace in Christ alone. This was a confession of faith and as Latimer listened, God spoke to his heart. He recalled Paul's conversion on the road to Damascus and began to compare himself with Paul before his conversion. His anxiety would not be hidden and Bilney pointed him to the Lamb of God Whose blood cleanseth from all sin and Whose work of redemption is "finished" and complete. Later in life, Latimer declared, "I learned more by his confession than before in many years." Bilney was later burned as a heretic at Norwich.

Latimer the zealous Roman Catholic was now a zealous Protestant and soon became one of the leading English Reformers. He was appointed Bishop of Worcester in 1535. His episcopate only lasted four years, for in 1539 he was compelled to resign because of his opposition in the House of Lords to the Six Articles prepared by the Duke of Norfolk with the King's approval and with the aim of reuniting the Church and healing divisions. These Articles, also known as "the whip with Six Strings" and "the bloody Statute," reasserted the fundamental beliefs of Roman Catholicism.

For the next eight years Latimer lived in retirement and under a cloud of suspicion. He spent the last year of Henry the Eighth's reign in the Tower of London. When Edward VI came to the throne Latimer was at once released and treated with respect. His old Bishoprick was offered to him; but this he declined. His constant friend throughout these testing years was Archbishop Cranmer.

The early death of Edward VI and the accession of Queen Mary to the throne in 1553, marked the end of Latimer's labours on behalf of the Gospel. He was arrested, imprisoned in the Tower, tried and finally burned at the stake, at Oxford, near Balliol College, on 16th October, 1555, in company with Bishop Ridley. As the flames rose around them, Latimer turned to Ridley and said, "Be of good comfort, brother Ridley, and play the man; we shall this day light such a candle, by God's grace, in England, as I trust never shall be put out." Before he died, Latimer cried, "Father of heaven, receive my soul!"

The candle which Latimer helped, by God's grace, to light, has burned ever since. Sometimes it has burned low; but it has never been extinguished. Its light brought blessing to countless thousands, not only in England but across the world.

JOHN CALVIN

❖

John Calvin was the second son of Gerard and Jeanne Calvin. He was born on 10th July, 1509 in the cathedral city of Noyon in France. Although Calvin spent much of his life in Geneva, Switzerland, he was brought up in the land of his birth - France. His mother died when he was very young and he was cared for in the home of a nobleman in the neighbourhood. Thus, while of humble stock (his grandfather had been a boatman on the river Cise), Calvin had social advantages over Luther in that in early life he moved easily in aristocratic circles and received a liberal education which fitted him for the position he as later to occupy in the Protestant Church throughout Europe.

Calvin was always a serious boy with a hunger for learning, and his father at first decided to prepare him for the Church, but later, considering the legal profession more lucrative, he changed his purpose. His father as secretary to the local bishop had used his influence to obtain for his son a benefice in the cathedral of Noyon, when John was aged 11 or 12. Shortly afterwards he sent him to Paris, to the College de la Marche, to prepare himself to read for the degree in Arts. At the age of 19 Calvin entered the University of Orleans, noted for its teaching of law. There he met two men who were to have a profound influence upon him in later years, Melchior Wolmar and Theodore Beza. Wolmar, a German, is thought to have been the first man to explain to Calvin the gospel of Jesus Christ as set forth in Scripture. He advised Calvin to abandon the study of Law and read Theology instead. In 1531 Calvin's father died and he was free to follow his deepest conviction that he should become a theologian. However in 1533 he did earn his degree of doctor of law.

Philip Schaff points out that "Calvin received the best education - in the humanities, law, philosophy and theology - which France at that time could give." He studied in the three leading universities of Orleans, Bourges and Paris from 1528 to 1533. He was so brilliant a student that he occasionally supplied the place of the professors! But he undermined his health, suffering from severe headaches, dyspepsia and insomnia.

During these years Calvin showed no trace of opposition to the Roman Catholic system and, as in the case of Saul of Tarsus, a brilliant career opened before him. He might have been a philosopher, lawyer or priest. Then suddenly, he embraced the cause of the Reformation and cast in his lot with a despised and persecuted sect. Certainly reformation was in the air. In France this was more so in the educated and upper classes. The clergy opposed the new opinions and men of letters defended them. King Francis I persecuted the Protestants and his sister, Marguerite d'Angouleme, queen of Navarre, protected them. There was ferment and agitation everywhere. Calvin, a devout Roman Catholic of upright character and serious disposition, could not be indifferent to such a clash of beliefs.

How and exactly when he was converted we do not know. But his conversion was dramatic and sudden. He refers to his experience in his Preface to his Commentary on the Psalms:

> Since I was too obstinately devoted to the superstitions of Popery to be easily extricated from so profound an abyss of mire, God by a sudden conversion subdued and brought my mind to a teachable frame, which was more hardened in such matters than might have been expected from one at my early period of life. Having thus received some taste and knowledge of true godliness, I was immediately inflamed with so intense a desire to make progress therein, that although I did not altogether leave off other studies, I yet pursued them with less ardour.

Calvin's conversion was, to quote Schaff, "a change from Romanism to Protestantism, from papal superstition to evangelical faith, from scholastic traditionalism to Biblical simplicity." He attributed this change exclusively to God and mentioned no human agency: "God ... subdued ... my mind."

Calvin's whole life and training before his conversion equipped him and marked him out as the leader and teacher of the evangelical party. People came to him from far and near seeking the truth. In vain he tried to escape them. God's hand had been laid upon him and later he was to write:

> As David was taken from the sheepfold and elevated to the rank of supreme authority; so

> God having taken me from my originally
> obscure and humble condition, has reckoned
> me worthy of being invested with the hon-
> ourable office of a preacher and minister of
> the gospel.

Calvin's seal of the flaming heart on the extended hand bore the Latin motto. *Prompte et sincere in opere Domini.* That he lived always ready to act "promptly and sincerely in the work of the Lord" cannot be denied. In his vast and indefatigable labours his sole concern was for the glory of God. Even his enemies respected him. In later years the French philosopher and rationalist, Ernest Renan - no friend of Calvinism! - described Calvin as "the most Christian man of his genera-tion." This Christian man, whose consuming passion was the glory of God, expressly forbade all pomp at his funeral or the erection of any monument over his grave, requesting that he be buried in a simple pine coffin and that no words be spoken at his grave - directions which were scrupulously observed and which were consistent with the gospel he loved and taught, a gospel that humbles man and exalts God.

ALEXANDER HENDERSON

❖

Alexander Henderson was a native of Fife in Scotland. He was born at or near the village of Luthrie in the parish of Creich, some time in 1583. Little is known of his parentage. He appears on the stage of history on 19th December, 1599, when, at the age of 16, he matriculated at St. Salvator's College in the University of St. Andrews, where he eventually obtained the degree of M.A.

Henderson proved an outstanding student and his abilities were recognised when he was appointed a Professor of Philosophy, a position he occupied until 1611. During this period he also completed his course in Divinity and he was probably influenced by Andrew Melville (the great leader of the Presbyterians in Scotland), who taught at St. Andrews until 1607. However, Henderson was at first strongly anti-Presbyterian in his views.

About 1613 or 1614, Henderson was preferred by the Archbishop of St. Andrews to be minister of Leuchars, a quiet country village some six miles north-east of St. Andrews. This strongly Presbyterian congregation did not want him and on his ordination day he found the door of the church nailed against him and he and his colleagues were forced to break into the building by one of the windows!

A few years later, Henderson went in disguise to hear Robert Bruce preach, being drawn to him, as Alexander Smellie tells us, much as Augustine was first attracted to Ambrose, simply by the fame of his oratory. As Ambrose was used to instruct Augustine, so Bruce became God's messenger to Henderson. Bruce pronounced his text with great emphasis: "Verily, verily, I say unto you, He that entereth not by the door into the sheepfold, but climbeth up some other way, the same is a thief and a robber." It came as a sword-thrust to Alexander Henderson. Smellie writes: "It seemed to the listener as if Christ were in the pulpit, searching him with reproachful eyes, and reproving him in the accents of a righteous Judge for his intrusion into a sphere to which he did not belong." This was the turning point in his life. He was spiritually aroused and returned to Leuchars a different man, penitent, believing and fully dedicated to Christ as Lord. He now gave his full support to that Presbyterianism which once he had despised.

The struggle with episcopacy was now well under way and Henderson moved steadily to the forefront of the battle. He was soon regarded by friend and foe as one of the chief leaders in the crusade against prelacy. His most significant contribution to the cause of Christ in Scotland was his involvement in preparing the drafts of the covenants of 1638 and 1643. He was, in fact, the chief author of the National Covenant of 1638 and the Solemn League and Covenant of 1643. Henderson ranks with John Knox and Andrew Melville, two of the most

distinguished sons of the Scottish Church. He was the states-
man of Scottish Presbyterianism. As a scholar and theologian,
he was unmatched. His holiness of life equalled all his other
qualities. He was respected by all who knew him as without a
trace of self-seeking and above all he was honoured as one
who loved Christ and His Kingdom. He was the first named
commissioner, empowered along with several others like
Samuel Rutherford and George Gillespie, to represent the
Church of Scotland at the Westminster Assembly of Divines.
In preaching, debate, travel and writing, Henderson spared no
pains in furthering the testimony of Scotland's Second Reformation.

In the summer of 1646, Henderson felt ill and weak. The
call came on the 16th August. He was ready and eager to go.
"Never schoolboy more longed for the breaking-up," he cried,
"than I do to have leave of this world." At the next meeting of
the General Assembly of the Church of Scotland, Henderson's
close friend, Robert Baillie, paid this tribute to him:

> "May I be permitted to conclude with my
> earnest wish, that the worthy memory of that
> glorious soul, who is now crowned with the
> reward of all his labours for God and for us,
> may be fragrant among us, as long as free
> and pure Assemblies remain in this land,
> which I hope shall be till the coming of the
> Lord. You know how he spent his strength,
> wore out his days, and did breathe out his
> life in the service of God and of this Church.
> This binds it on us and posterity to account
> him the fairest ornament, after John Knox of
> incomparable memory, that ever the Church
> of Scotland did enjoy."

RICHARD CAMERON

❖

Richard Cameron was born about 1648 in the old
Fifeshire town of Falkland. His parents, Allan Cameron
and Margaret Paterson, were sober, God-fearing Scots.
His father was a merchant in Falkland and represented the best
of a diligent middle class to which Scotland owed a great deal.
There were two younger sons, Michael and Alexander (who
became a Covenanting minister) and a daughter, Marion, who
is said to have died at the hands of the troopers.

Richard was brought up an Episcopalian and when he
had taken his University degree, he found a position as school-
master in Falkland under the Episcopal curate. At this time he
began to attend field meetings conducted by the Covenanters
and one day he was caught in the Gospel net along with many
more. He underwent a radical change, being truly converted.
From that day he turned his back on Prelacy and found his

spiritual home with the Presbyterians and, as Alexander Smellie puts it, "showed himself a root-and-branch man." The conversion of Cameron was a momentous event both for himself and for the Kingdom of God in Scotland.

Soon Cameron associated himself with the great covenanting preacher, John Welsh, then holding field meetings at Teviotdale. Welsh persuaded a very reluctant Cameron to accept licence as a preacher and in due course he was sent to the difficult district of Annandale. As Cameron hesitated Welsh declare, "Go your way, Ritchie; set the fire of hell to their tail."

God blessed Cameron's ministry from the outset. But he was outspoken and fierce in his denunciations and it became necessary for John Welsh and some colleagues to meet with Cameron and lovingly reprove him for a zeal which was not always according to knowledge. A few months later he crossed to Holland and soon his voice was heard preaching the Gospel in the Scots Kirk at Rotterdam. Here, too, he received ordination, which would have been difficult for him to have obtained in Scotland at that time.

At his ordination Cameron was addressed by Robert MacWard who said: "The public standard of the Gospel is fallen in Scotland, and if I know anything of the mind of the Lord, ye are called to undergo your trials before us, and go home and lift the fallen standard, and display it before the world, But, before ye put your hand to it, ye shall go to as many of the field ministers as ye can find, and give them your hearty invitation to go with you; and if they will not go, go your lone, and the Lord go with you." As his hand rested on Cameron's head, MacWard cried, "Behold! all ye spectators. Here is the head of a faithful minister and servant of Jesus Christ, who shall lose the same for his Master's interest; and it shall be set up before sun and moon in the public view of the world."

MacWard's words came to pass much sooner than could have been anticipated. In October 1679 Cameron was back in Scotland to "lift the fallen standard of the Gospel". Nine months later his earthly race was over and yet so greatly was he used by the Lord that his name stands for ever emblazoned on the pages of Scottish history. He was called "the Lion of the Covenant" and no wonder, for he was enthusiastic and dauntless in espousing the Crown Rights of his Royal Saviour.

On the 22nd June 1680, just a year after the defeat of Bothwell Brig, some men on horseback rode into the burgh of Sanquhar. Two of them dismounted and walked to the Cross. They were Richard and Michael Cameron. As the people gathered around, a psalm was sung; prayer was offered; and then Michael read a paper, the famous Sanquhar Declaration. This Declaration disowned Charles Stuart and his reign and pledged allegiance to the Lord Jesus Christ. It described Charles as a tyrant and usurper and "all the men of his practices, as enemies of our Lord Jesus Christ and His Cause and Covenants." When the document was read, it was nailed to the Sanquhar Cross. Battle had been joined and obviously Cameron's life was now in danger; indeed there was a high price on his head, dead or alive.

On the night of 21st July, Cameron slept in the farmhouse of William Mitchel in meadowhead at the Water of Ayr. It was to be his last night on earth. Next afternoon he and his small band of men saw the dragoons sent by Dalzell to search for him. They met at Ayrsmoss, a lonely stretch of mossy ground. As they prepared to stand and fight, Cameron gathered his men for prayer. Three times he cried, "Lord, spare the green, and take the ripe!" But in his own case the green was not spared. The Lion of the Covenant fell in battle when no more than thirty-two years of age.

The dragoons cut off Richard's head and hands and brought them to his old father, Allan Cameron, then a prisoner in the Tolbooth for supporting the conventicles near his own town of Falkland. Showing the grisly remains to the prisoner, they asked, "Do you know them?" Allan Cameron bent over and kissed them and said, "I know them! I know them! They are my son's my dear son's." And then weeping and praising God at the same time, he added, "It is the Lord! Good is the will of the Lord, Who cannot wrong me nor mine, but has made goodness and mercy to follow us all our days."

It was a great day for the Kingdom of God in Scotland when Richard Cameron was converted. He was a noble soul, a passionate preacher of the Gospel, a true patriot, utterly loyal to his Saviour and Lord. He was ready to hazard all for a land in covenant with God. It was that concern which prompted the Sanquhar Declaration and which led to his early martyrdom. He stands in the front rank of that noble army of martyrs who "overcame by the blood of the Lamb, and by the word of their testimony; and ... loved not their lives unto the death."

JOHN BUNYAN

❖

John Bunyan was born in 1628. He first saw the light of
day in a labourer's cottage in the village of Elstow, a mile
from Bedford. His father worked in his forge and so John
Bunyan became known as the "tinker's son from Bedford!"
An old print of the cottage where John was born shows a shed
at the side, described as "the forge," and this lends support to
the view that Bunyan's father plied the honourable trade of
smith. However Bunyan did refer to what he termed his "low
and contemptible descent in the world."

Bunyan's parents had the sense to send him to school,
where he learnt to read and write. As a young lad he was soon
to be found in bad company and he devoted himself to licen-
tiousness. He was terrible profane. "It was my delight," he
wrote, "to be taken captive by the devil at his will: being filled
with all unrighteousness: that from a child I had few equals -

both of cursing, swearing, lying and blaspheming the holy name of God." It would seem that his parents did nothing to check his downward career. Yet there were times when his conscience smote him. "The Lord," he wrote, "even in my childhood, did scare and affright me with fearful dreams, and did terrify me with dreadful visions." Still he continued on his evil way. "I was the very ringleader of all the youth that kept me company, into all manners of vice and ungodliness."

During those wild, godless days, Bunyan nearly lost his life on several occasions. Once he almost drowned in the sea. Another time he fell out of a boat in Bedford river and nearly perished. On another occasion, in an encounter with an adder, he struck out with a stick, stunning the creature, and then proceeded to force open its mouth and tear out the sting with his bare fingers, a desperate and dangerous act. Later he joined the army at about eighteen years of age (probably the royal army and not Cromwell's "praying and preaching Roundheads!"), where he found much evil company. On one occasion he was chosen to go on a military mission and another soldier asked to take his place. Bunyan agreed and the one who replaced him was later shot in the head and died. Bunyan later declared: "Here were judgments and mercy, but neither of them did awaken my soul to righteousness, wherefore I sinned still and grew more and more rebellious against God, and careless of mine own salvation."

At the age of twenty, Bunyan married. He did not choose a woman as hardened as himself, but a lady who was virtuous, loving, born of godly parents who had instructed her in the truth. One of his biographers comments that "he must have been a persuasive lover to have gained so good a helpmate, and she a confiding young woman, to run the risk of being so unequally yoked." His wife had two books the "Plain Man's Pathway to Heaven," and the "Practice of Piety." She persuaded

John to read these books and go to Church. Quietly, lovingly, patiently this woman influenced her husband for good and so he began to have fears concerning his salvation, wondering at times if he might have sinned away the day of grace. Yet he still plunged from time to time into depravity and shame.

One day as Bunyan was uttering the most appalling oaths, he was rebuked by a woman of loose morals, who said that she trembled to hear him swear and curse in such a fashion. She told him that he was the "ungodliest fellow she had ever heard, and that he was able to spoil the youth in a whole town." Public reproof from such a person struck home like an arrow and Bunyan vowed reformation of life. Reformation there was, but no spiritual renewal. His conversion came about in the most unexpected way. He overhead some Christian women in conversation about the mercy of God, their love of Christ and deliverance in time of temptation. They spoke with obvious joy. In that moment Bunyan realised that despite his new-found morality, he was not a Christian. "At this I felt my own heart begin to shake, as mistrusting my condition to be nought; for I saw that in all my thoughts about religion and salvation, the new birth did never enter my mind; neither knew I the comfort of the word and promise ..." And so began a tremendous internal struggle. The Holy Spirit of God was dealing with this remarkable man - a man who must either hate God with all his heart or love Him with all his heart.

After weeks of anguish, Bunyan sought out the women in Bedford whom he had overheard discussing spiritual things. They were Baptists and their pastor was the godly John Gifford. Gifford began to instruct Bunyan and so the poor, burdened sinner found himself in the company of Evangelist. For about a year Bunyan's anguish increased and terrible were the battles that raged in his soul. But peace and joy finally flooded his being as he rested in Christ. Now he had a sudden yearning to speak to others of his Saviour. He could not contain himself. "I thought I could have spoken of His love and of His mercy to me, even to the very crows, had they been capable to have understood me." His struggles and doubts were by no means over (read his "Pilgrim's Progress"), for Satan would not easily leave him alone. But he was a new creation in Christ Jesus and as such he joined the fellowship of the Baptist church in Bedford, to which the godly women who had been such a help to him belonged, and under the ministry of Mr. Gifford he was strengthened in his faith and instructed in the doctrines of grace.

We have not space to give a detailed account of his remarkable conversion, or to tell of the subsequent life and labours of this man whom Christ saved: but as we reflect upon his experience we can only praise God for His mighty grace so wondrously displayed in the salvation of John Bunyan. As we scan the three large volumes of his works, we realise that the Church of Christ would be immeasurably the poorer without them. Only eternity will reveal the blessing received by tens of thousands of the Lord's people through reading Bunyan.

MATTHEW HENRY

❖

Matthew, the second son of Rev. Philip Henry, was born on 18th October, 1622 at Broad Oak, a farm house in the township of Iscoyd in Flintshire, some three miles from Whitchurch in Salop. Rev. Philip Henry was a nonconformist minister of considerable piety and scholarship. His wife, Katherine, is described as a "woman of uncommon excellence" and her distinguished son, Matthew, remarked that "in her sphere and capacity, she was not inferior to what his father was in his." As a child, Matthew experienced the pressure of intolerance, for it was in the year of his birth that about two thousand faithful ministers of the gospel, including his father were separated form their congregations by the Act of Uniformity.

During infancy and childhood, Matthew's health was delicate, although at a very early age he gave indications of exceptional mental ability and a studious disposition. At the age of ten he was reduced by a slow fever to the brink of the grace and his parents feared they were going to lose him. The boy recovered and began to show what one of his biographers describes as "an uncommon seriousness of disposition in one so young." He spent much time alone in his room and clearly the Spirit of God was working in his young heart and mind.

The details of Matthew Henry's conversion are given in one of his manuscripts dated October 18, 1675, entitled, "Catalogue of Mercies". In this document he writes, " Lord Jesus I bless Thee for Thy Word, for good parents, for good education, that I was taken into covenant betimes in baptism; and, Lord, I give Thee thanks, that I am thine, and will be thine." He continues, "I think it was three years ago that I began to be convinced hearing a sermon by my father on Psalm 51: 17, 'The sacrifices of God are a broken spirit; a broken and a contrite heart, O God, thou wilt not despise.' I think it was *that* that melted me; afterwards I began to enquire after Christ." On December 7, 1673 Philip Henry preached on the marks of true grace. Matthew tried himself by then and told his father of the evidences of repentance and faith. "He liked them, and said, if these evidences were true (as I think they were) I had true grace." The marks that confirmed Matthew in his conviction that he was now a child of God were as follows: "covenant transactions between God and the soul," true repentance for sin and true love for God, including God's Word and God's people.

It is interesting to see the emphasis that he laid on what he termed "covenant transactions between God and the soul." Indeed it is astounding to find a lad who was not quite eleven years old attaining to a profound theological insight into the nature of conversion as being essentially covenantal, when many devout and mature Christians either fail to see this or refuse to believe it. Matthew had no legalistic or contractural view of covenant response. His words on the matter are crystal clear: "There is true conversion where there have been covenant transactions between God and the soul. And I found that there have been such between God and my soul, and I hope in truth and righteousness. If I never did this before, I do it now; for I take God in Christ to be mine. I give up myself to be His in the bond of an everlasting covenant never-to-be-forgotten. But hath it been in truth? As far as I know my own heart, I do it in truth and sincerity. I did it December 7th, and September 5th, and October 13th, and many other times. I do it everyday." Matthew never lost sight of this vital aspect of Christian experience. In is "Communicant's Companion," he describes the Lord's Supper, amongst other things, as "a covenanting ordinance" and writes, "We do in and by this ordinance seal to Him, to be to Him a people. We accept the relation by our voluntary choice and consent, and bind our souls with a bond, that we will approve ourselves to Him in the relation. We hereby resign, surrender, and give up our whole selves, body, soul and spirit, to God, the Father, Son and Holy Ghost, covenanting and promising that we will by His strength serve Him faithfully, and walk closely with Him in all manner of gospel obedience all our days. Claiming the blessings, of the covenant, we put ourselves under the bonds of the covenant, O Lord, truly I am thy servant, I am thy servant; wholly, and only, and for ever Thine. And this is the meaning of this service."

The striking and beautiful thing about this remarkable lad's conversion, which he so clearly saw as a covenant response to God's Covenant of Grace, was the instrumentality of his father's faithful preaching. He was much moved by that ministry, and listened to his father's sermons with intense interest, often withdrawing afterwards to his room to reflect and pray. It was from his father that he sought counsel and help and as Matthew's biographer, J. B. Williams, puts it, "What greater joy could such a man as Philip Henry have had than to hear his son, his only son, thus early enquiring for the way to Zion! And how unspeakable was the privilege of the son to possess in his father a scribe well instructed in the doctrine of the kingdom of heaven ..."

Matthew followed in his father's footsteps and became a minister of the gospel, labouring for Christ in Chester and Hackney. He was a good preacher, but his reputation rests mainly upon his celebrated commentary on the Bible. It was begun in 1704. He lived to complete it only as far as the end of the Acts. The commentary is outstanding for its devotional value and in this respect has never been surpassed. It was completed by a number of ministers - Henry's contemporaries. George Whitefield made constant use of Henry's commentary, read it through four times and always referred to its author as "the great Mr. Henry".

Matthew Henry's many other works have not received the attention they deserve, especially his "Directions for Daily Communion with God", "The Communicant's Companion," "A Treatise on Baptism," "A Method for Prayer," "A Scripture Catechism," (largely an exposition of The Shorter Catechism of the Westminster Divines) and his biography of his father.

Matthew Henry died on 22nd June, 1714. He was essentially a man of the Word. "Call the Bible your glory," he wrote, "and dread its removal. Phinehas' wife when the ark was taken, named her child Ichabod - the glory is departed. Part with all rather than your Bibles."

JOHN WESLEY

❖

John Wesley was born at Epworth on June 28th, 1703. His family had been traced back to a period before the Norman Conquest. His father, Samuel Wesley, married Susannah, the twenty-fifth child of Dr. Samuel Annesley. She became the mother of nineteen children, John Benjamin being the fifteenth. Samuel Wesley was a graduate of Oxford and a minister of the Church of England. The rectory at Epworth was burned when John was six years old, and his escape made a deep impression on his mind. He spoke of himself as "a child of Providence."

With a large family and a small income Samuel Wesley had difficulty in keeping the proverbial wolf from the door and John was reared in stringent circumstances. Susannah Wesley undertook the early eduction of her children. At the age of ten, John was admitted to the Charterhouse School,

London. He entered Christ Church College, Oxford, some years later and was ordained in 1725, elected fellow of Lincoln College in the following year and given the degree of M.A. in 1727. He served his father as curate for two years and then returned to Oxford in 1729 to fulfil his functions as fellow. That same year saw the beginning of the rise of Methodism. The famous "Holy Club" was founded at Oxford - also called the Reforming Club, Bible Moths, Enthusiasts and the like! It included John and Charles Wesley and its members were derisively nicknamed "Methodists" because of their self-discipline and methodical habits.

At this stage in his life John was deeply religious, although there were periods of laxity. He was much impressed by Law's "Serious Call" and gave himself more fervently to a strict and abstemious life. He responded to missionary needs in Georgia, where he felt a certain burden for the Indian population. However his High Church leanings and strict enforcement of ecclesiastical rules, and especially his preaching against the slave trade and gin traffic, made him unpopular with the colonists and he returned to England in 1738.

Before commencing missionary work with the Moravians, Wesley was interviewed by a Mr. Spangenberg, a Moravian minister. Spangenberg asked, "Does the Spirit of God bear witness with your spirit that you are a child of God?" Wesley did not know how to reply. He was then asked, "Do you know Jesus Christ?" And he replied, "I know He is the Saviour of the world," "True," said the minister, "but do you know that He has saved you?" Wesley answered, "I hope He has died to save me," Later Wesley was to write, "I, who went to America to convert others, was never myself converted to God."

Wesley had close associations with the Moravians, and from them he had learned that true faith was inseparably connected with a sense of peace proceeding from the knowledge of the forgiveness of one's sins. For years Wesley had struggled against sin and endeavoured to produce righteousness of life and to know peace, but in vain. This was because, as he later put it, he sought it not by faith but "by the works of the law." It was at a Moravian meeting in Aldersgate Street, London on May 24th, 1738, as he listened to the reading of Luther's Preface to the Epistle to the Romans, that Wesley came to experience saving faith. As he listened to Luther's explanation of faith and the doctrine of justification by faith, Wesley suddenly saw and understood. "I felt," he wrote, "my heart strangely warmed. I felt I did trust in Christ, Christ alone, for salvation; and an assurance was given me that He had taken away **my** sins, even **mine**, and saved **me** from the law of sin and of death."

From that time the Methodist movement grew, and soon its leaders, particularly the Wesleys and Whitefield, were persecuted by clergymen and magistrates. The doors of churches were closed against them. They were forced to preach in the open-air. Soon they were used by God to bring about a great awakening in England at a time of much spiritual darkness and moral declension. Wesley rode on horseback all over the land, preaching often twice and thrice a day, and was described as "the busiest man in England."

Wesley was a strong controversialist. The most notable of his controversies was that on Calvinism. In this he followed his father's thinking and consequently found himself in conflict with his fellow Methodist, George Whitefield, who was a staunch Calvinist. Yet when Wesley preached at Whitefield's funeral, he proclaimed nothing that Whitefield would not have heartily endorsed.

Bishop Ryle's assessment of John Wesley is charitable and accurate: "If I am asked whether I prefer Whitfield's gospel to Wesley's, I answer at once that I prefer Whitefield's: I am a Calvinist and not an Arminian. But if I am asked to go further and to say that Wesley preached no gospel at all, and did no real good, I answer at once that I cannot do so. That Wesley would have done better if he could have thrown off his Arminianism, I have not the least doubt; but that he preached the gospel, honoured Christ and did extensive good, I no more doubt than I doubt my own existence." Ryle concludes, "He was a bold fighter on Christ's side, a fearless warrior against sin, the world, and the devil, and an unflinching adherent of the Lord Jesus Christ in a very dark day. He honoured the Bible. He cried down sin. He made much of Christ's blood. He exalted holiness. He taught the absolute need of repentance, faith, and conversion ... Let us thank God for what John Wesley *was*, and not keep poring over his deficiencies, and only talking of what he *was not*. Whether we like it or not, John Wesley was a mighty instrument in God's hand for good; and, next to George Whitefield was the first and foremost evangelist of England in the 18th century.

Wesley went home on March 2nd 1791.

GEORGE WHITEFIELD

❖

George Whitefield was born in Gloucester in the month of December, 1714. His ancestry was quite distinguished, the Whitefield family having had a relationship with Oxford University for several generations and with the ordained ministry of the Church of England. George's father, Thomas Whitefield, served his time to the wine trade in Bristol and eventually entered business for himself, obtaining the proprietorship of the Bell Inn at Gloucester. He was just nineteen years of age and at that time he married Elizabeth Edwards, a Bristol girl of the same age. She came from a good background and her father was in the trade of manufacturing cutlery.

During their years at the Bell, Thomas and Elizabeth Whitefield had seven children: first there were five boys, then a girl and finally a boy - George. Thomas's promising business career was cut short by an early death at the age of thirty-five. At that time George was just two years old.

Brought up in a comfortable middle class home, George was in many ways a privileged lad; although it may be noted that due to neglect on the part of his nurse at a time when he had measles, he contracted a permanent mis-focus of his eyes, which later left him with a squint. Later in life, when his stand for Biblical truth made him unpopular in some circles, his detractors referred to him as 'Doctor Squintum.'

Comfort and privilege do not guarantee good character. In his 'Journals' Whitefield writes: "I can truly say I was froward from my mother's womb. I was so brutish as to hate instruction and used purposely to shun all opportunities of receiving it ... I soon gave pregnant proofs of an impudent temper. Lying, filthy talking, and foolish jesting I was addicted to ... Sometimes I used to curse, if not swear. Stealing from my mother I thought no theft at all, and used to make no scruple of taking money out of her pocket before she was up ... It would be endless to recount the sins and offences of my younger days. They are more in number than the hairs of my head. My heart would fail me at the remembrance of them, was I not assured that my Redeemer liveth, ever to make intercession for me."

This does not mean that George was a particularly evil boy. He wrote this account when he was sensitive to the heinousness of sin and at a time when he enjoyed much popularity and he was anxious to extol the grace of God in his life, He was, as Arnold Dallimore puts it, "in all probability ... much like his brothers and playmates, and was simply what one might expect of a lad frowing up in an inn during an exceptionally dissolute age." Dallimore reminds us that a public house "is seldom a savoury place in which to bring up a child, but in the early days of the eighteen century it could hardly have failed to abound with evil ... It was in this environment with its unavoidable familiarity with the ways of sin that George Whitefield spent the first sixteen years of his life."

When George was eight years old his mother remarried. Her new husband, Capel Longden, came of good stock and hopes were high. But soon it became apparent that the marriage was a failure. Longden's management of the inn and possibly his demeanour, saw a falling off in trade and eventually the business was in a precarious state. Finally Elizabeth separated from him and obtained a cottage of her own. George joined her later.

Because of reduced circumstances it seemed that his hopes of going to Oxford, in the family tradition, would not be realised. Then, when not yet seventeen, his dream became a possibility. A young man who had been to Oxford told him how he had been able to defray his expenses by working in the University as a servitor. There were provisions at Oxford for undergraduates of limited means to wait on the Fellows and other gentlemen at table and to perform various menial tasks: this was accepted as part payment of college fees. Whitefield went as a servitor to Pembroke College, Oxford.

Just before going to University, Whitefield came across Law's "Serious Call," but had not the money to buy it. Later, at Oxford, he saw it again and this time managed to procure it. He tells in his "Journals" that as he read this little book, "God worked powerfully upon his soul." At this time he came under the influence of the Wesleys and began to associate with "the despised Methodists". He adopted a disciplined and religious way of life, but knew nothing of salvation by grace. As a member of "the Holy Club," of which John Wesley was leader, he practised regular devotions, partook of the Sacrament, fasted each Wednesday and Friday and kept Saturday as a day of preparation for the Lord's Day. He was introduced to much good reading. He became increasingly dissatisfied with his spiritual state and bean to search for life. This search took the form of increased bodily austerities, which in turn only increased his anguish and fear. His work began to suffer, as did his health. His physician ordered him to bed, where he lay for seven weeks. He had come to the point of despair. Then God revealed Himself in mercy to Whitefield. He had spent many hours reading his Greek Testament and in prayer. One day, in great distress and desperation, he cast his soul on the mercy of God in Christ and immediately he found peace. "God," he wrote, "was pleased to remove the heavy load to enable me to lay hold of His dear Son by a living faith, and by giving me the Spirit of adoption, to seal me even to the day of everlasting redemption. O! with what joy - joy unspeakable - even joy that was full of, and big with glory, was my soul filled, when the weight of sin went off ... " Later he wrote: "I know the place! It may be superstitious, perhaps, but whenever I go to Oxford I cannot help running to that place where Jesus Christ first revealed Himself to me and gave me the new birth."

Whitefield soon became a leader among the Methodists. He was a staunch Calvinist and the most striking orator of the Methodist revival. His vast labours included several visits to America. He may not have been as good an organiser as the Wesleys, but "his influence in awakening the religious conscience of the 18th century went very deep" (Oxford Dictionary of the Christian Church). His labours wore down his health and he died at the relatively early age of fifty-five. His strong convictions and burning zeal were matched by his tolerance and catholicty of spirit. He was no bigot. He had a forgiving and loving disposition. This is, perhaps, best illustrated by his request, made shortly before his death, that John Wesley should be asked to preach at his funeral. There had been prolonged and intense controversy between these two men about the doctrines of Calvinism, but as Bishop Ryle tells us, Whitefield regarded Wesley as Calvin did Luther, "only as a good servant of Jesus Christ." Ryle also records the moving incident when a censorious Christian asked Whitefield if he expected to see John Wesley in heaven. "No, sir," was the striking reply, "I fear not. He will be so near the throne, and we shall be at such a distance, that we shall hardly get sight of him." Whitefield died in New England on Sabbath 30th September, 1770. Charles Wesley in his "Elegy on Whitefield" wrote:

"And is my Whitefield enter'd rest?
With sudden death, with sudden glory, blest?

•••

He speaks - and died! transported to resign
His spotless soul into the hands divine!
He sinks into his loving Lord's embrace,
And sees his dear Redeemer face to face."

DAVID BRAINERD

❖

David Brainerd was born on April 20, 1718 at Haddam
in Connecticut, New England. He was born into a distinguished family, his father, Hezekiah Brainerd,
being one of his Majesty's council for the colony. On his mother's side there were long standing associations with the gospel
ministry. David was the third son in a family of five sons and
four daughters. He tells us in his *Diary*, "I was from my youth
somewhat sober, and inclined rather to melancholy ... but do
not remember any thing of conviction of sin till I was, I
believe, about seven or eight years of age. Then I became concerned for my soul, and terrified at the thoughts of death ..."

For a period he showed some interest in spiritual things,
attended worship and "said" his prayers. In 1732 the outbreak
of a fatal illness in his area aroused David, now in his early
teens, to a greater sense of his need. He became more fervent

in his religious duties and even hoped that he was a Christian. Clearly the Holy Spirit was dealing with him and when his mother died in 1732 he was much distressed. But once again his anxiety subsided and he felt secure in a round of religious activities. As yet there was no real repentance or trust in Christ alone for salvation.

Brainerd as a lad in his teens was, as he put it, and not unnaturally, "addicted to young company", but these associations were not spiritually helpful and he often returned from what was termed "frolicking" with an uneasy conscience. Spiritually he was depending on self-righteousness: that lay at the heart of his religious life. He had the husk without the kernel, the externals without the inner reality that they symbolised and were meant to express. He became increasingly strict in his religious observance, going to extremes. By the age of twenty and now living in Durham, N.C., he had ceased associating with other young people, read his Bible avidly, - "more than twice in less than a year" he records - listened earnestly to the sermons, trying to recall them before retiring for the night. Even on Monday mornings he often practised recalling the sermons of the previous day! If mere religion could have saved anyone, and if earnestness and sincerity could have helped, then David Brainerd would have been that person. All along, he tells us, he had "a secret hope of *recommending* himself to God" by his religious duties. But any peace that came to him by these means was short-lived and his distress only increased.

Brainerd was so much in earnest about his salvation that in February 1739 he set apart a day for fasting and prayer and he "spent the day in almost incessant cries to God for mercy". That day did enable him to realise his helplessness and his sinfulness and undoubtedly he was near to the kingdom, but still he had not found peace. He seemed for a period to alternate between times of great conviction of sin and times of sluggishness. God's Spirit did not leave him in peace. He tells, for example, how one night when out for a walk, "I had opened to me such a view of my sin that I feared the ground would cleave asunder under my feet, and become my grave; and would send my soul quick into hell, before I could get home." That night he was so fearful that he could not sleep. Yet the devil had an interest in Brainerd too, and at times the lad tended to regard his times of conviction as in come way meritorious, and then he grew cold and languid again".

As time passed, Brainerd began to resent the ways of God. He writes that when in this frame of mind the corruption of his heart was especially irritated by four aspects of God's ways - the strictness of His Law, that salvation was by faith *alone*, that he found faith a mystery, and that God was sovereign in the salvation of sinners - he found Romans 9:21 particularly offensive. But his spiritual travail was about to end. He writes, "while walking in a solitary place ... I at once saw that all my contrivances and projects to effect or produce deliverance and salvation of myself, were utterly in vain; I was brought quite to a stand, as finding myself totally *lost*." That was the turning point for Brainerd. For several days he remained in this state of mind until gradually he began to see God in the light of His Word and the resentment that had prevailed for a time left him. This gave him much joy. Brainerd had earlier decided to prepare for the gospel ministry - all part of his effort to please God. Now, in 1739, he entered college, not without trepidation, and there, in due course, he experienced with many others the blessing of the Revival that came to a number of areas, including New-Haven where the college was.

Brainerd did not find full peace and assurance quickly or easily. There were times of depression and doubt, but God did bring him into the fulness of salvation in Christ.

Having completed his study of theology and been licensed to preach, Brainerd was later examined by the commissioners of the Society in Scotland for Propagating Christian Knowledge and appointed as their missionary to the Indians. Thus began his life's work as a pioneer missionary. God blessed his labours abundantly as he worked among the Indians and many were led to a saving knowledge of Christ, but that is an eventual story on its own. Brainerd had suffered from ill health for some considerable time yet persevered, often when very weak, in his missionary labours. He died of consumption on Friday, October 9th, 1747, at the early age of twenty-nine.

The conversion of David Brainerd is significant for several reasons. While some experience a gentle conversion like Lydia "whose heart the Lord opened", others, like Philippian gaoler, experience a sharp crisis (Acts 16:14, 27-31). Some find peace in a short space of time, others, like Brainerd agonise for months, even years, before entering into the assurance of salvation. The latter experience is painful, but it has one benefit, for, as JC Ryle comments, "what we win easily, we seldom value sufficiently. The very fact that believers have to struggle and fight hard before they get hold of real soundness in the faith, helps to make them prize it more when they have attained it". For years David Brainerd struggled to make himself fit for the Kingdom of God. It took him a long time to see that the sinner is saved by grace alone, through faith alone and in Christ alone. He had to learn that good works are the *fruit* of saving faith and not the *ground* of our salvation, and that there is no contribution of any kind that man can make to his salvation. Salvation is of the Lord. To be saved the sinner must abandon everything of self and rest solely in Christ for salvation. That cannot be said too often or too strongly.

Let not conscience make you linger,
Nor of fitness fondly dream. All the fitness He requireth
Is to feel your need of Him.

JOHN NEWTON

❖

John Newton was born in London on 24th July, 1725. His father was away at sea for most of his childhood and so John's upbringing was left to his mother. She is described by one of Newton's biographers as a "frail, sweet-natured, God-fearing woman." She faithfully taught her boy the Scriptures. The peace and happiness of the home were shattered when John's mother died in 1732. His mother had longed for her son to enter the gospel ministry and had often commended him in earnest prayer to God. His father remarried and the new Mrs. Newton had little love for her stepson and no interest in his spiritual welfare. There were no more Bible stories and prayers before bed, and John was allowed to mix freely with godless children and soon became like them.

At the age of eleven, John was taken on his first voyage by his father, a captain in the Mediterranean trade routes. His father was severe and distant and John was left to find his company with the sailors, who were often coarse and profane. He grew like them. On at least two occasions he was arrested in his downward way, once when, at the age of twelve, he was throne from a horse and narrowly escaped being impaled on some stakes, and again when he missed by just a few minutes a long-boat that was to take him and a friend to visit a man-of-war; the boat overturned and his friend was drowned. Strangely enough, Newton could not swim.

Sometimes his conscience would smite him as he recalled the instruction received at his mother's knee and then he would attempt a measure of reform and spend time reading his Bible and in prayer. Such occasional religious exercises brought him no peace.

Space forbids a detailed account of Newton's dramatic career. The salient features of his life before conversion include falling in love at the age of seventeen with Mary the fourteen year old daughter of Mr and Mrs. Catlett, who had nursed his mother in the closing days of her life (she became his wife some six years later), being press-ganged into service on a man-of-war at the age of nineteen and seeing action against French warships, desertion from his ship with the consequent savage punishment, eventual discharge from the Navy and service as a slave-trader along the West African coast. Newton had become a hardened infidel, rejecting God, morality and truth. At the age of twenty-three he is said to have been "little removed from the state of a wild animal". In his auto-biography, Newton describes his life at that time as "sinning with a high hand."

The first thing that really brought Newton to his knees was a violent Atlantic storm. It was on the night of 10th March, 1748, that a howling gale battered his vessel, the Greyhound, and tossed it like a cork between thirty-foot waves that crashed on the shuddering deck. It was a night of terror. A man was swept overboard before his eyes. The ship seemed in imminent danger of sinking. For ten days the Greyhound wallowed in dangerous sees and John Newton began to fear death and to despair of mercy. His mouth refused to utter his customary oaths and blasphemies.

Lashed to the helm, with his feet braced against the heaving deck, Newton had time to think. The review of his life was not pleasant. He recalled his debauchery and profanity and felt that he had forfeited forgiveness. It was then that his mother's instruction came back to him. He found himself repeating Proverbs 1: 24-31. That passage begins, "Because I have called, and ye refused; I have stretched out my hand, and no man regarded; but ye have set at nought all my counsel, and would none of my reproof: I also will laugh at your calamity; I will mock when your fear cometh."

The storm passed and the ship was saved, but a tempest continued to rage in Newton's heart. Gradually his thoughts turned to Christ and His death on the cross. He began to read the New Testament. The days passed and the stricken vessel limped into Lough Swilly in Co. Donegal - almost a picture of Newton limping home to God, still struggling with fears and doubts. Making his way to Londonderry, he began to attend church regularly. As the time for Communion drew near, he earnestly renounced his sin and sought mercy at the Saviour's hand. He had became a "new creature". It is probably safe to say that his conversion experience lasted from the night of the storm until this moment.

This is how Newton describes his preparation for his first Communion: "At length the day came. I rose very early, was very particular and earnest in my private devotion, and with the greatest solemnity, engaged myself to be the Lord's forever, and only His. This was not a formal, but a sincere surrender, under a warm sense of mercies recently received. For want of a better knowledge of myself, and the subtlety of Satan's temptations, I was later seduced to forget these vows. However, though my views of gospel salvation were very indistinct, I experienced a peace and satisfaction in the ordinance that day to which I had been hitherto a perfect stranger."

Newton's clearer understanding of the gospel and assurance of salvation came later. The greatest change in his life occurred between 1750 and 1754. He decided to enter the ordained ministry of the Church of England, and after some difficulty was ordained in 1764. His mother's prayers had been answered. He obtained the curacy of Olney in Buckinghamshire, where he became the close friend of the poet William Cowper. Later Newton became rector of St. Mary Woolnoth and lived to a ripe age: he died on 31st December, 1807. He was a popular preacher and soon became the leader of the Evangelical party in the Church of England, enjoying much fellowship with nonconformist ministers as well as with those of the Establishment. He was on good terms with Wesley and Whitefield.

Newton used his pen to good effect and his writings include letters entitled "Omicron" and "Cardiphonia." He also wrote some fine Christian verse, including the poem which begins -

> Amazing grace! how sweet the sound!
> That saved a wretch like me;
> I once was lost, but now am found;
> Was blind, but now I see.
>
> 'Twas grace that taught my heart to fear,
> And grace my fears relieved;
> How precious did that grace appear,
> The hour I first believed!

That was the experience of "the old African blasphemer," as he called himself in his last days.

The epitaph on Newton's monument was prepared by himself is characteristic. "John Newton, clerk, once an infidel and libertine, a servant of slaves in Africa, was, by the rich mercy of our Lord and Saviour Jesus Christ, preserved, restored, pardoned and appointed to preach the faith he had long laboured to destroy."

> 'Tis grace has brought me safe thus far,
> And grace will lead me home.

WILLIAM COWPER

❖

William Cowper, the poet, was born in the rectory of
Great Berkhampstead, in Hertfordshire on 26th
November, 1731. He came of what used to be
termed "gentle blood." His father. Dr. John Cowper, was chap-
lain to George II, and his grandfather was a judge and brother
of the First earl Cowper, the Lord Chancellor. His mother, Anne,
was the daughter of Roger Donne of Ludham Hall in Norfolk,
a descendant of Dr. Done the famous poet and satirist. Cowper's
mother died in 1737 at the age of thirty-four, leaving, of
several children, only two sons surviving. William, the eldest,
was then six years old.

The same year that he lost his mother, William was sent
to a large boarding school in Hertfordshire, where a Dr. Pitman
was head master. A delicate and timid child, he suffered much
at the hands of a bully aged fifteen, who treated him savagely.

This situation was finally discovered and the bully was expelled.

When still quite young, the boy showed a constitutional tendency to melancholy and was often in low spirits. Later he studied at Westminster School, where he had such companions as Warren Hastings, and at the age of eighteen he was sent to study law with Mr. Chapman, an attorney. But he wasted time and, as he himself, put it, was "constantly employed from morning to night in giggling and making giggle, instead of studying the law." Incidentally, his fellow giggler, Edward Thurlow, later became Lord Chancellor of England! In 1754, Cowper was called to the bar and appointed Commissioner of Bankrupts in 1759. He was, however, more interested in literature than law. When his income proved to be insufficient, he was nominated Clerk of Journals to the House of Lords, but the nomination was disputed and he was required to submit an examination. The nervous dread of this ordeal unsettled his reason, a condition aggravated by certain losses and disappointments. His friend, Sir William Russell, was drowned while bathing in the Thames and his uncle, Ashley Cowper, flatly refused him permission to marry his daughter, Theodora, who was much beloved by Cowper and who returned his affection. It was then that this young man wrote:

Doomed as I am in solitude to waste
The present moments, and regret the past;
Deprived of every joy I valued most,
My friend torn from me, and my mistress lost:
See me neglected on the world's rude coast,
Each dear companion of my voyage lost;
Nor ask why clouds of sorrow shade my brow,
And ready tears wait only leave to flow;
Why all that soothes a heart from anguish free,
All that delights the happy, palls with me.

His moods changed rapidly. Shortly after penning the above lines he joined the Nonsense Club, a small group of Westminster men, who dined together every Thursday! But melancholy was his prevailing mood and on one occasion he even attempted suicide and almost succeeded. This was followed by a conviction of sin, coupled with a sense of God's wrath and a deep despair of escaping it. His mind became so unhinged that he was taken to St. Albans, where a Dr. Cotton kept a house for such patients. Here, in July 1764, and burdened with a sense of sin, he opened a Bible that had been left for him to read and the first verse he saw was Romans 3: 25, "Whom God hath set forth to be a propitiation through faith in His blood, to declare His righteousness for the remission of sins that are past, through the forbearance of God." In that moment he believed and received the gospel. He was overwhelmed with a sense of love and wonder, and joy flooded his soul. Some time later, at Huntingdom, near Cambridge, Cowper heard a sermon on the parable of the Prodigal Son and he saw himself reflected so clearly, and the loving kindness of his sighted Lord so vividly, that the whole scene was, to quote one biographer, "acted over his heart." Yet his constitutional tendency to acute depression remained and reappeared more viciously than ever before in 1773. Cowper sensed the approach of this dark cloud and wrote:

> God moves in a mysterious way
> His wonders to perform;
> He plants his footsteps in the sea,
> And rides upon the storm.

When the storm came it was terrible. It is hard to believe that the author of the poem, "Oh! for a closer walk with God," wrote during this period, "My thoughts are clad in sober livery

... They turn, too, upon spiritual subjects; but the tallest fellow, and the loudest among them all, is he who is continually crying with a loud voice ... 'All is over with thee; thou art lost.'"

In 1767, Cowper had moved to Olney, where he lived a stone's throw from he home of Rev. John Newton, for whom he was to act as "law assistant". They became fast friends, and Newton, the converted slave-trader, had a profound and beneficial influence upon him. The charge that Newton's "religiosity" was largely responsible for Cowper's mental state, a charge made, for example, in "Encyclopaedia Britannica," is palpably absurd, for his malady was deep-seated from early days. At Olney (a name associated with Newton, Cowper and Scott the commentator), Cowper wrote a considerable amount of sacred verse in addition to his more general poetic labours. His religious poetry is evangelical and theologically robust. There is considerable reference to the blood of Christ, possibly because of his conversion experience, and although occasionally crude, these references are always doctrinally sound and frequently sublime.

The struggle between faith and fear, hope and despair, is apparent in his religious verse.

> The billows swell, the winds are high,
> Clouds overcast my wintry sky;
> Out of the depths to thee I call,
> My fears are great, my strength is small.
>
> Tho' tempest-toss'd and half a wreck,
> My Saviour thro' the floods I seek:
> Let neither winds nor stormy main,
> Force back my shatter'd bark again.

Many similar examples could be given; yet when we take the broad sweep of his writing, faith dominates, not fear. Hope always emerges victorious. The same man wrote:

The dearest idol I have known,
Whate'er that idol be;
Help me to tear it from thy throne,
And worship only Thee.

So shall my walk be close with God,
Calm and serene my frame;
So purer light shall mark the road
That leads me to the Lamb.

Cowper could pray most movingly. Someone remarked, "Of all the men that I ever heard pray, no one equalled Mr. Cowper." He was a distinguished correspondent. The poet Southey called him "the best of the English letter-writers." "Encyclopaedia Britannica" states that "he ranks among the half dozen greatest letter writers in the English language."

Apart from their artistry these letters display considerable good taste and wisdom. To his friend of later years John Johnson, he wrote, "My Dearest of all Johnnies, I am not sorry that your ordination is postponed. A year's learning and wisdom added to your present stock, will not be more than enough to satisfy the demands of your function."

Cowper was dogged by bouts of extreme dejection to his dying day. He died on 25th April, 1800 and later a memorial window was placed in Westminster Abbey in honour of George Herbert and William Cowper, two of England's most outstanding sacred poets.

In the opinion of the writer, Cowper was not mad. He stumbled along that strange borderline between genius and madness. Assurance often forsook him and we would do well to remember the statement in our Confession of Faith that "true believers may have the assurance of their salvation divers ways shaken, diminished and intermitted ... yet are they never utterly destitute of that seed of God, and life of faith, that love of Christ and the brethren, that sincerity of heart, and conscience of duty, out of which, by the operation of the Spirit, this assurance may, in due times be revived; and by the which, in the meantime, they are supported from utter despair." The Church of Christ would have been much the poorer without the work of this sweet, sensitive soul, whose whole experience may be condensed in that single cry, "Lord, I believe; help thou mine unbelief."

WILLIAM CAREY

❖

William Carey was born in 1761 in the village of Paulerspury, near Towcester in Northamptonshire. His parents, Edmond and Elizabeth Carey, were weavers, working at the loom in their own home. It was a home where God was loved and honoured. From an early age it became clear that William was a bright boy who would do well at school and when in his sixth year his father, Edmond Carey, was appointed master of the free school in the village, his son had advantages that other children of his age lacked. William's sister, Polly, wrote "when William was in his sixth year he discovered a great aptness for learning". His father commented, "He was always attentive to learning when a boy, and a very good arithmetician". William as a lad was adventurous and he was keenly interested in Nature - birds, flowers, trees all fascinated him. His love of learning knew no bounds. In his teens he had mastered Latin. He was a prodigious reader, and books of science, history and travel were of special interest.

Such a boy could not be indifferent to the claims of religion. Carey had read the Scriptures from earliest days. He was familiar with the Psalms and Lessons used in church which he attended regularly. But he comments, "Of real experimental religion I scarcely heard anything till I was fourteen years of age: nor was the formal attendance upon outward ceremonies, to which I was compelled, a matter of choice". He disliked books on religion, with one exception, Bunyan' *Pilgrim's Progress* - this he read "with eagerness, though to no purpose".

Sadly, as he grew older, Carey found the wrong companions and became like them. "I was addicted to swearing, lying and unchaste conversation ... and though my father laid the strictest injunctions on me to avoid such company, I always found some way to elude his care". Yet he was unhappy in sin. His home training and the early although unrecognised working of the Holy Spirit in his heart filled him at times with a sense of loathing in the midst of evil.

Carey's father did not choose for him weaving as an occupation - that home craft was now threatened by new machinery. Instead he entered him for a seven year apprenticeship to shoemaking. His master in the trade was Clarke Nichols - a man with a hot temper and a tongue to match. Carey had as a fellow apprentice another local lad, John Warr. Warr was already concerned about his own spiritual state. His grandfather had been a co-founder of the local Independent church. Carey despised Dissenters. Their children were excluded from the nearby school. His father and grandfather had been staunch Anglicans and Carey would gladly have burned down the meeting-house where John Warr worshipped.

John Warr did come to a saving knowledge of Christ and immediately witnessed to Carey. He lacked Carey's skill in debate. But even when Carey seemed to have triumphed he had failed to convince himself and he experienced a growing uneasiness. The young Dissenter was wielding a two-edged sword and Carey felt its thrust.

In 1779 Carey approached a crisis in his life. The American War was at its height and the Established Church supported the war on the colonists. Carey was opposed to this policy and was to that extent out of sympathy with the church. On January 11th a national day of prayer was held in response to the royal appeal. Carey listened to a sermon by Thomas Chater, an independent preacher from Olney. Words from Hebrews 13:13 moved him deeply - "Let us therefore go forth unto him without the camp, bearing his reproach". He felt a strong desire to follow Christ. This was probably the year of his conversion.

At this period England was experiencing revival through the preaching of the Wesleys and Whitefield. While there is no evidence that Carey ever heard any of these men, it would have been most unusual if he had not been influenced indirectly by this movement of the Spirit. Wesley visited Carey's neighbourhood eighteen times and when he preached in Whittlebury, he was only a mile and a half from Carey's home.

During this same period Carey sometimes went to hear Rev. Thomas Scott, curate of Ravenstone, who afterwards became famous as a biblical commentator. Many years later Carey wrote, "If there be anything of the work of God in my soul, I owe much of it to his [Scott's] preaching when I first set out in the ways of the Lord". Carey could never give a precise date for his conversion, but clearly God used different men to bring the challenge of the Gospel to him at a time of great personal need: his conversion was more a process than a crisis.

Although he owed so much to the ministry of Thomas Scott, Carey became a Nonconformist. At this time a number of "Particular Baptist" ministers in Northamptonshire and adjacent counties formed an Association of Fellowship and Christian Service. Soon Carey got in touch with them and before long he was accepted as a faithful preacher of the Word. And so a maker of *soles*, to use a Shakespearean pun, became a winner of *souls*. He turned again to the study of languages and became proficient in Latin, Greek, Hebrew, and Italian - and then he turned to Dutch and French! No wonder Thomas Scott, who knew Carey well, refereed to the shoemaker's cottage as "Carey's College".

This was the man who was largely responsible for the formation of the Baptist Missionary Society in 1792 - he was then 31 years of age. His clarion cry was, "Expect great things from God: attempt great things for God". This, too, was the man, who after two pastorates at home, set sail for India, with his wife, on June 13th, 1793. This was the beginning of his outstanding service as a pioneer missionary for some forty years.

As an evangelist, teacher, and translator, William Carey did monumental work in India - to translate Scripture into eleven different tongues is no mean achievement. Well has he been called "the father of modern missions". To read the story of his life's work is an enriching experience. Carey died at sunrise on June 9th, 1834. For him it was the sunrise indeed. In accordance with the directions contained in his will, his gravestone was simply inscribed -

WILLIAM CAREY

Born August 17, 1761, Died June 9th, 1834.

A wretched, poor and helpless worm,

on Thy kind arms I fall.

In all the annals of missionary endeavour, since biblical times, it is doubtful if anyone was more greatly used by God than William Carey.

BILLY BRAY

❖

B illy Bray was born at Twelveheads, a tin-mining village near Truro, Cornwall, on June 1, 1794. His paternal grandfather worshipped in the Methodist chapel, which he had helped to build. Billy's father was also a devout Methodist. He died when his children were very young and Billy lived with his grandfather until he was seventeen years old. He then moved to Devon. Here he married and here, too, he lived a wild life of drunken debauchery. Later he said, "I became the companion of drunkards, and during that time I was very near hell." During those reckless days he had a number of hairbreadth escapes from death. Once, when working in the mine, he heard a rent in he overhead rock and began to run. Forty tons of rock fell on the spot where he had been working. On such occasions he was sobered in spirit, but only for a short time. Yet conscience often troubled him. "I used to dread to go to sleep," he said, "for fear of waking up in hell."

After seven years in Devon, Billy returned to Cornwall a confirmed drunkard. His wife had to go out nightly and fetch him home from the public house. "I sinned against light and knowledge," he said, "and never got drunk without being condemned for it." He often reflected, in later life, on his evil youth. He kept bad company, but remarked, "I was the worst of the lot." So terrible was his blasphemy that his godless companions declared "that his oaths must come from hell, for they smelt of sulphur"!

Billy Bray was an eccentric and a wit. He could ridicule holy things and often did so. Later, as a Christian, this same wit was to make him popular as a witness to others. At the age of twenty-nine, Billy came under real conviction of sin as the result of reading Bunyan's "Visions of Heaven and Hell." Bunyan describes two lost souls in hell cursing each other, for being the author of each other's destruction and noted that they who love one another on earth, may hate one another in hell! Billy thought of his closest drinking companion. Like an arrow the thought struck him, "Shall S. Coad and I, who like each other so much, torment each other in hell?"

Billy's wife had been converted when young, but had become a backslider before marriage. Secretly Billy longed for his wife's restoration, thinking that this would make conversion easier for him. That was not what happened. Billy's burden grew so heavy that he arose from his bed one morning at three o'clock and began to pray. "I found," he said, "that the more I prayed, the more I felt to pray."

For some days Billy wrestled in prayer and spent much time reading the Bible. He was in obvious distress, so that even his fellow-workers began to pity him. Billy's response was typical: "I was glad that I had begun to seek the Lord, for I would rather be crying for mercy than living in sin." Peace finally came to him as he knelt alone in his room. Here is how he describes that moment... "I said to the Lord, 'Thou hast said, They that ask shall receive, they that seek shall find, and to them that knock the door shall be opened, and I have faith to believe it.' In an instant the Lord made me so happy that I cannot express what I felt. I shouted for joy. I praised God with my whole heart for what He had done for a poor sinner like me; for I could say, The Lord hath pardoned all my sins. I think this was in November, 1823, but what day of the month I do not know. I remember this, that everything looked new to me, the people, the fields, the cattle, the trees. I was like a man in a new world. I spent the greater part of my time praising the Lord. I could say with Isaiah, 'O Lord, I will praise Thee, for though Thou wast angry with me, Thine anger is turned away, and Thou comfortedst me;' or like David, 'The Lord hath brought me up out of a horrible pit of mire and clay, and set my feet upon a rock, and established my goings, and hath put a new song in my mouth, even praise unto my God.' I was a new man altogether."

Billy's sanctified eccentricity and wit immediately came into service, as he witnessed to all whom he met and told what the Lord had done for his soul. "Some said I was mad: and others that they should get me back again next payday. But, praise the Lord, it is now more than forty years, and they have not got me yet. They said I was a *mad*-man, but they meant I was a *glad*-man, and, glory be to God! I have been glad ever since." The exuberant man could also be tremendously serious. Often, before going down the mine with the other men, he would remove his cap and pray aloud, "Lord, if any of us must be killed or die today, let it be me; let not one of these men die, for they are not happy; but I am, and if I die today I shall go to heaven."

Billy Bray was instrumental in times of revival in Cornwall and many were led to seek the Saviour through his preaching and testimony. Before conversion, the public house had been his haven; now he hated it with "a perfect hatred". Public houses, he said, were "hell houses" for they were places "where people were prepared for hell." Having been a drunkard himself, he knew that "moderation" was no cure. "Ye might as well hang an old woman's apron in the gap of a potato field to prevent the old sow with young pigs from going in, as expect a drunkard to be cured with moderation."

Billy Bray's wife was spiritually restored soon after his conversion and he was used of God in bringing this to pass. Together they rejoiced in God's goodness and mercy. Billy's life was marked by real happiness. He was constantly praising God and constantly exhorting others to seek the Saviour. His religion was intensely practical and many testified to his personal interest and kindness. He simply bubbled over with joy. "I am the son of a King" was one of his favourite sayings. Few, if any, have shown so much of the joy of salvation as Billy Bray; and few, if any, have been as faithful in personal witnessing.

This is how the Rev. M. G. Pearse described Billy Bray's religion: "Religion to Billy was not a duty to be done - not a privilege to be enjoyed in leisure hours - not a benefit club, a comfortable provision for 'rainy days' - it was a **life**. Never left behind, never put off with the Sabbath's clothes, never hidden before great of low, good or bad, but **in** him, flowing through him, speaking in every word, felt in every action, seen in every look - deep, true, abiding religion was with him altogether a life. Dead indeed unto sin, he was now living unto God through Jesus Christ."

Billy was almost seventy-four when he died after preaching at Crantock in May 1868. There was a revival in progress at Crantock, and Billy, although very tired and looking like a man in the last stages of consumption, was actively involved.

When the doctor examined him, Billy asked, "Well, doctor, how is it?" "You are going to die," was the grave reply. Billy shouted, "Glory! glory be to God! I shall soon be in heaven." Then, in a low voice he asked, "When I get up there, shall I tell them you will be coming too?" So he witnessed to the end. His last word was "Glory!" Thus there stepped into eternity one of the worst and one of the best men, and one of the happiest of the saints of God.

> High on the hills of Eden,
> With angels on the wing;
> Shouting his favourite saying,
> "I AM THE SON OF A KING!"
> Climbing the dew-clad mountain
> Of God's eternal truth,
> In all the vigour of manhood,
> In all the beauty of youth.

There is a sense in which the experience of conversion agrees with the personality in question, as "this man and that man" enters Zion. This was certainly so in the case of a rough Cornish stone which, when cut and polished by the Spirit of God, flashed with a lustre all its own. Were Billy Bray to guide our pen in closing this brief sketch of his experience of grace, he would have us write but one word - Hallelujah!

GEORGE MULLER

❖

George Muller was a native of Prussia, born near Halbertstadt on September 27th, 1805. His father was a customs official. George had no proper parental training; his father's favouritism toward him was harmful, leading to jealousy and estrangement within the family. Too much pocket money resulted in waste and indulgence. Soon George learned to steal and practice deceit and when found out and punished, he devised more cunning methods of fraud. By the age of ten he was an habitual thief and a clever cheat.

Muller's father wished his boy to become a clergyman and before he was eleven he was sent to the cathedral classical school at Halberstadt to prepare for university. It would seem that his father simply regarded the ministry of the Gospel as a profession rather than a divine calling. From this time the lad's studies were mixed with card-playing, drinking and other vices. The night when his mother lay dying, George was staggering along the streets drunk: not even her death aroused him, in fact he drew steadily worse.

In due course Muller was confirmed, withholding from the clergyman responsible for his preparation a large part of the confirmation fee entrusted to him by his father. He was confirmed in the spring of 1820, but, alas! in reality he was confirmed in sin, being unregenerate and immoral and quite ignorant of saving truth.

In November 1821, Muller went to Magdeburg to study in the cathedral school there, and then to Brunswick where he fell in love with a Roman Catholic girl. In his absence from home, he took one downward step after another, wasting his money and sinking deeper and deeper into sin. Finally at the age of sixteen, he was sent to jail for fraud. He was now a hardened swindler, drunkard and companion of criminals. His father's anger a this time was so great that Muller outwardly reformed his ways and took pupils in subjects as German, French and Latin. For several years he studied classics and earned a measure of respect. But at heart he was no different. In his library of over three hundred books there was not a copy of the Bible, but writers like Moliere and Voltaire he knew and valued. Yet twice a year he went to the Lord's Supper and then he would sometimes vow to change his ways, but Satan had taken him captive at his will and Muller was utterly helpless.

This was the man who was not only admitted to the honourable standing as a university student, but also accepted as a candidate for the Gospel ministry, a student in divinity quite ignorant of God and His salvation! He was not happy. Expediency and policy urged him to amend his ways, but there was no distaste for sin and no repentance. Besides, he was now suffering from illness due to his debauched lifestyle.

It would take many pages to describe, even in outline, Muller's astounding career of evil and shame - nearly twenty years of wickedness. One Saturday afternoon about the middle of November 1825, his friend Beta, a backslider, told Muller that the was going that evening to a meeting in a friend's house. Muller felt a desire to go too, although he could not tell why. Perhaps he was aware of his own wickedness and his lack of peace. That evening proved to be the turning point in his life. He was in the home of J. V. Wagner in Halle. There he heard a man praying for God's blessing on the meeting and this made a deep impression upon him. God's Word was read and expounded. Muller listened attentively and that night in his room he knew that God had spoken to him and he found peace. As yet his eyes were but half opened, as though he saw men as trees walking; but Christ had touched those eyes and Muller was a new man. Someone stronger than Satan had set him free.

In 1829 Muller came to London to take up an appointment for the Society for Promoting Christianity among the Jews. Forced by ill-health to leave London, he moved to Teignmouth where he associated himself with the Brethren movement and became a preacher. Two years later he moved to Bristol where he devoted his life to the care of orphan children, relying on voluntary contributions and praying to God to meet the need. He began with only a few children and eventually had two thousand under his care, accommodated in large houses at Ashley Down, near Bristol.

At the age of seventy, Muller left this work in the hands of his daughter and her husband, and set out with his second wife on a preaching mission to Europe, America, India, Australia and China - a tour which lasted over seventeen years! He died in Bristol in 1898 at the age of ninety-three. What a conversion! The profligate youth had become a preacher of the Gospel and a Christian philanthropist. But that is not all.

His "Narrative of the Lord's Dealings with George Muller" was widely circulated. In 1857, a young Irishman,

James McQuilkin, recently converted at a time when God's Spirit was working noticeably in his locality, read the first two volumes of that Narrative. He said to himself, "Mr. Muller obtains all this simply by prayer; so may I be blessed by the same means," and he began to pray. His first answer was a spiritual companion and then two more of like mind. They met for prayer in a small schoolhouse near Kells, Co. Antrim, every Friday evening. In answer to their prayers a farm-labourer was converted and then there were five! Soon there were six. A fire had been kindled through prayer and so began one of the most widespread and memorable revivals of the nineteenth century, the 1859 revival, when thousands found Christ. George Muller was converted in a prayer meeting in 1825. Who said, "Only one conversion"?

J. C. RYLE

❖

John Charles Ryle was born on 10th May, 1816, the fourth child in a family of six children. As he himself puts it, "I was born on May 10, 1816, at 4 o'clock in the morning at Park House near Macclesfield, in the county of Cheshire." His father John, was married to Susanna, a cousin of Sir Richard Arkwright, the inventor. The family home was at Macclesfield, in the Peak district of England, where the Ryles (thought originally to have been Royle) had been long established. J. C. Ryle's father had inherited a large fortune made in silk, and was a member of the House of Commons for the Borough of Macclesfield. He increased his wealth from his holdings as a banker and landlord and it has been estimated that his annual income (in Victorian times) was between fifteen and twenty thousand pounds. His business failed in 1841 as a result of mismanagement on the part of a subordinate and he lost his entire fortune in a day.

As a child John showed signs of having a sturdy intellect and a contemplative mind. Once a guest in his home found him alone by the window and asked what he was thinking about. The boy replied, "I am meditating about an elephant!" He had the blessing of a happy home, his "most searing memory", to quote from one of his biographies, was that of "being washed in a wooden tub every Saturday night and having his hair combed with a fine tooth comb." Preparatory school at Helmingham Hall, which Ryle entered at the tender age of eight, proved to be primitive, brutal and academically deficient. He left this school in 1827, afterwards stating that he had learnt more evil during his short time there than he had done in the rest of his life. "A boy's first school," he wrote, "is a turning point in his life." He added that he left school, "tolerably well grounded in Latin and Greek, but having learned a vast amount of moral evil and got no moral good."

Ryle entered Eton in 1828. There he found that "most of the boys knew far more about heathen gods and goddesses than about Jesus Christ." He did appreciate the discipline of Eton. He left Eton in 1834 and before going to Oxford, had a holiday in Ireland with the Cootes of Ballyfin. He was on friendly terms with all three brothers at Eton, mainly because of their fondness of cricket. He went with one of the Cootes on a visit to Cork. His chief memory of Cork was that of falling asleep in the Cathedral during the sermon!

Ryle's great love as a lad was cricket. He was captain of his team at Eton in the match against Harrow, and he led the Oxford side in his three seasons as a University representative. He excelled himself in the match with Cambridge in 1836 and he also won a place in the Oxford Eight which rowed against the Light Blues. This love of sport remained with him throughout his life. He came third in the much coveted Newcastle Scholarship where he was a Sixth Form boy at Eton.

This scholarship was based on a programme of study which made Theology for the first time a school subject in its own right. This was to prove significant in Ryle's career. Later he wrote, "I shall always thank God for what I learned then." Ryle distinguished himself academically, winning several important scholarships. He took so brilliant a First in the Humanities on his graduation in 1838 that it was said that the Examiners regarded him and two others as being in a class by themselves.

We have, then, a young man with an outstanding athletic and scholastic record, coupled with the advantages of a pleasing personality and family wealth. It would seem that the ball was at his feet. Yet Ryle was not satisfied and a change was taking place in his inner life. In his wealthy home the things of God were held in respect, but there was a lack of devotion to Christ. The family lived a life of ease. Later in life Ryle wrote: "Up to the time that I was about twenty-one years old, I think I had no true religion at all. I do not mean to say that I did not go to church, or was not a professed Christian: I had no infidel or R.C. opinions, but I think I was perfectly careless, thoughtless, ignorant and indifferent about my soul, and a world to come. I certainly never said my prayers, or read a word of my Bible, from the time I was seven to the time I was twenty-one."

Ryle had refused to be influenced by the ritualist Tracatarian Party which was active in Oxford during his time there. As one of his biographers put it, "he was too masculine in mind and character to be satisfied with vagaries and sophistries of this order." In the mid-summer of 1837 Ryle was taken seriously ill and for a time was left weak in body. God was speaking to him. For some months he experienced mental conflict. The crisis came on a Sabbath morning early in 1838. He entered an Oxford church after the commencement of the service and was just in time to hear the Second Lesson.

It was taken from the second chapter of Ephesians. As he heard the words, "For by grace are ye saved through faith; and that not of yourselves: it is the gift of God." The voice of God seemed to be speaking to him. Only at that moment did he fully grasp the gospel of grace. It was the moment of his conversion.

Ordained in 1841, Ryle rose in his Church to become Bishop of Liverpool from 1880-1900. These were the crowning years of his life and work. A strong evangelical, he preached a pure gospel, wrote extensively and took a strong stand against Romanist encroachments in the Church of England. His warnings with regard to Romanist tendencies now seem prophetic. His tracts have been printed and distributed throughout the world in tens of thousands and are still unequalled for their simplicity, directness and Biblical content. Ryle died on 10th June, 1900, but his ministry continues through the printed page (at present most of his works are in print) and his name is still revered wherever the Evangelical Faith is treasured.

DAVID LIVINGSTONE

❖

The Livingstones had been for generations a humble and deeply religious people. David Livingstone's grandfather tilled a small farm on the Island of Ulva, not far from Oban in Scotland. The Livingstone family was forced to move south as part of a slow exodus from the West Highlands, as small crofters were being compelled to make way for sheep. As one of Livingstone's biographers, James I. Macnair, put it, "Sheep paid better and gave a surer return, so the people had to go." The Livingstones came to Blantyre, outside Glasgow, where Neil Livingstone found employment in the mill of a certain David Dale. His son, also Neil, became apprenticed to a tailor, David Hunter, a god-fearing man.

Neil junior disliked the tailoring trade and soon left it, but he stayed long enough to marry his employer's daughter in 1810. For a time they lived in Anderston, Glasgow, where their first child died. They returned to Blantyre and on March 19, 1813, David was born.

From his earliest days David was bookish. A farmer who occasionally employed him to herd his cattle, remarked in later years, "I didna think muckle o' that David Livingstone when he worked wi' me. He was aye lyin' on his belly readin' a book." Livingstone's biographer, Macnair, comments that it is easy to see how those hard-worked, practical folk would have little time for a boy who "wandered about by himself, had no interest in games and girls as other lads had; who was always reading and would spend his spare time scouring the country collecting 'bits o' flo'ers and bits of stanes and sic like trash.'"

Times were hard in David's boyhood. Those were the days of slump after the Napoleonic wars. David had to enter the mill at the early age of ten. His upbringing was tough and demanding. The mill bell woke him in the morning at 5:30. He would pull on his few scanty garments, sup a plate of porridge and rush off to the mill with its noise and humid atmosphere. He was known as a "piecer" and his job was to tend the spinning jenny and tie up the broken threads. The work was light and he had time to learn his Latin grammar. That book of Latin grammar may still be seen at the Livingstone Museum at Blantyre. It is recorded that the mill girls took delight in tossing bobbins at the book which he kept perched on his machine! There were two people in particular who recognised the possibilities in David. One was Mr. McSkimming, a teacher; the other was an Irish lad, named Gallacher, later a well known Roman Catholic priest in Partick. Gallacher helped David with Latin.

David spent twelve years in the mill. During that time he read widely and well. Books that were readily available included Boston's "Fourfold State" and "Marrow of Modern Divinity." David was familiar with these, but gradually he turned his attention to books on science and travel. He later stated that the last time his father used the rod on him was when he refused to read Wilberforce's "Practical Christianity", a best seller in its time. This unnecessary severity only served to increase David's distaste for doctrinal reading and his father being suspicious of scientific books, a coolness arose between them. It was age the age of 20, however, that David read Dr. Thomas Dick's "Philosophy of a Future State," a book which proved instrumental in his conversion. David had seen science and religion in conflict. Dick showed him that they were not hostile to each other but rather complementary. His conversion was unemotional, yet mind and heart were inevitably involved as he quietly bowed to Christ as his Saviour and Lord.

About this time Livingstone read a pamphlet by Karl Gutzlaff of the Netherland Missionary Society, in which the author appealed for medical missionaries to go to China. Livingstone decided to be such a missionary. After attending theological and medical classes at Glasgow, he offered his services to the London Missionary Society, was provisionally accepted and then pursued a further course of study. In 1840 he passed at Glasgow as Licentiate of the Faculty of Physicians and Surgeons. It seems that he seriously jeopardised his chances by arguing with his examiners about the use of the stethoscope!

Livingstone's last night at home was indelibly etched upon his memory. In later years, as he tramped across Africa, he would recall that cosy room, his mother with tears of joy in her eyes, his aged father trying to look stern in order to hide his emotions, his brother and sisters, the reading from the big family Bible and the singing of the 121st Psalm.

On November 20, 1840, Dr. Livingstone was ordained as a missionary in Albion Chapel, London, and two weeks later, on December 8th, he sailed to Africa. His partner in life was to be Mary Moffatt, eldest daughter of the famous Dr. Robert Moffatt, on whose mission station at Kuruman he first worked. An earlier romance had withered in the bud.

Livingstone's conversion was in no sense dramatic, but it was tremendously real in his experience - a true, evangelical conversion which proved that God's Spirit had graciously worked in his heart. The genuineness of this conversion is reflected in the prodigious labours of his life as a pioneer missionary, and while he was undoubtedly an intrepid explorer and a capable scientist, Livingstone was primarily and essentially a Christian missionary. His famous exploratory journey across Africa lasted just under four years, during which time he covered, mostly on foot, a distance of six thousand miles.

On the morning of May 1, 1873 Livingstone was found dead, kneeling at his beside, in the attitude of prayer. His devoted African attendants buried his heart under a large Mulva tree. His mortal remains were eventually buried in Westminster Abbey, on April 18, 1874, amid the profound grief of the whole nation. Among the mourners in the Abbey was his father-in-law, Dr. Robert Moffatt, who outlived him by ten years. So lived and died the mill boy from Blantyre.

He needs no epitaph to guard his name,
Which men will prize while worthy work is known.
He lived and died for good, be that his fame;
Let marble crumble: this is Living-stone.

MARY SLESSOR

❖

Mary Mitchell Slessor was born in Aberdeen in December 1848. That was the period in Scotland known as "The Hungry Forties". Crops had failed. A developing factory system had almost destroyed the old cottage industries. People moved in large numbers to the cities in search of work. Many were disappointed in their search and poverty and crime were rampant.

Mary was the second of a family of seven children. Her father, Robert, was a shoemaker and her mother, Mary was a weaver. When three of his children died, including his eldest son. Robert became an alcoholic. By 1859 he had drunk himself out of his job. His wife's wages of ten shillings for a fifty-eight hour working week were not sufficient to support the family so they moved to Dundee where the main industry was weaving.

Mary was ten years old when the Slessors came to Dundee. At that time there were over thirty thousand people living in one-room homes known as "single-ends". That was the accommodation the Slessors were obliged to accept. Her parents found work but between them they earned a pittance and the family eked out a bare existence in those terrible slums, referred to by one writer as "sunless rookeries."

Mary was sent to work in a mill as "a half-timer" while still a young child. A "half-timer" was a child whose time was divided between school and work in a mill. So at the age of eleven, Mary became a mill-lassie and had to rough it, growing up in an environment of poverty and degradation. Her journalist biographer. James Buchan, writes, "It would have been difficult for God or man to have found a better place than the slums of Dundee to prepare Mary for the conditions under which she was to work in Africa." We might put it somewhat differently, but we take his point. For in later years Mary was to move amid the most appalling cruelty and indescribable conditions of dirt, vermin and disease. The shocking conditions of her childhood made her tough, resilient and assertive. By the age of fourteen, Mary had developed into one of the toughest of her "breed", her nickname being "Carrots" because of her red hair, and "Fire," because of her quick temper! She was a natural leader, but hardly the type of person that one would consider to be a possible missionary.

Mary's mother had been deeply moved, during her time in Aberdeen, by an address given by a missionary on furlough from Calabar, West Africa. He told of the terrible conditions created by the slave trade and as she listened, Mrs. Slessor prayed inwardly that one of her sons would to Calabar as a missionary. She frequently borrowed the "Missionary Record" from her Church library and would read it to her children, who often played at teaching black children. In Mary's childhood "Calabar" was a household name. Never for a moment did Mrs. Slessor think that her daughter Mary, the local "Carrots" and "Fire" would make a missionary.

It was when Mary had become a "full-timer" in 1862, that God's purpose for her life began to unfold. An old widow who lived nearby was worried as she saw young girls, like Mary, exposed to the perils of slum life. She would invite them to sit on the floor in her cosy room and talk to them about the danger of their wild life. One evening she took Mary's hand and held it close to the fire. "If you were to put your hand in there, it would be awful sore," she said, "But if you don't repent your soul will burn in blazing fires for ever and ever." In later years Mary would smile when recalling that incident. At the time it made such an impression on her that it gave her nightmares. However it did cause her, for the first time, to think seriously about life and death and eternity and God. Could she really speak to Jesus? Would He hear her? She tried to do so and formed the habit of "chatting" to Him as she went about her duties. Then she began to read the Bible and to borrow books from the church library. To equip herself for further study, she enrolled for classes at night school two evenings a week. In her search for truth she was greatly helped by a new minister who had come to that United Presbyterian congregation, Rev. James Logie.

As her reading improved, Mary's keen mind began to grapple with the teaching of the New Testament. At the heart of that teaching she found Christ. Increasingly she was drawn to Him and to His royal service. Unlike that of Newton or Muller, her conversion was gradual, like that of Lydia, "whose heart the Lord opened."

Mary's hero was David Livingstone. She was twenty-five when Livingstone died in 1873. The Scottish newspapers were full of the story of his passing and how African servants had struggled for weeks to carry his body back to the coast. James Buchan writes, "Mary read the reports about her hero's death and a ridiculous idea began to come into her mind and to keep returning there as often as she threw it out: she was to follow Livingstone to Africa." Well, the "ridiculous idea" came to fruition. Thank God for ridiculous ideas! Perhaps it should be "praise God"! Mary eventually applied to the Foreign Mission Board of her Church in 1875, and to its credit the Board did not succumb to the all too prevalent short-sightedness and ecclesiastical inertia of the established denominations. The mill-girl was accepted, provided she continued to improve her education and this would include some study in Edinburgh at the Board's expense. On August 5th, 1876, Mary sailed on the "SS Ethiopia" for Calabar. From then until her death in 1915, she exercised considerable incfluence among the native population and succeeded in bringing to an end such tribal abuses as twin murder, human sacrifice, witchcraft and cruel punishments. In 1905 the Government, recognising her influence and authority, invested "Ma Slessor," as she was popularly known, with the powers of a magistrate.

Sad to say, Mary is now largely forgotten by her countrymen. They were reminded of her life and work, however, when Her Majesty Queen Elizabeth, on a visit to Nigeria, and at her own special request, placed a wreath on Mary Slessor's grave. James Buchan suggests that this may have been because of the Queen's Scottish childhood and describes this act as "a fitting tribute to one of the greatest Scotswomen who ever lived." We would add, "and one of the Lord's choicest saints." When R. M. McDonald showed a lantern lecture in the area where Mary had laboured, he finished with a picture of Mary herself. An old chief asked if he could keep the table cloth which had served as a screen and into which her face seemed to have faded. "She was my friend," he said, "and I like that face too much."

C. H. SPURGEON

❖

Charles Haddon Spurgeon was born at Kelvedon, Essex, on 19th June, 1834. He was the grandson of Rev. James Spurgeon (for many years pastor of the Independent Church at Stanbourne, Essex) and son of Rev. John Spurgeon, also an Independent minister and pastor of a congregation in Islington, London. When old enough to leave home, Charles was sent to stay at his grandfather's, remaining there until 1841 when he was sent to school in Colchester. There he acquired a reasonably good knowledge of Latin, Greek and French and was first in his class in every examination. In 1848 he spent several months in an agricultural college at Maidstone, conducted by a relative. In 1849 he became usher in a school at Newmarket, kept by a Baptist and he began to attend a Baptist church. An outbreak of fever in the school brought Spurgeon's first term there to an abrupt end and he returned home.

The influences brought to bear upon his young life had been good. His early home life, both at his father's and grandfather's, had been sheltered from evil. He was growing up, as he himself puts it, "a respectable lad." "I was not," he says, "like other boys - untruthful, dishonest, disobedient, swearing, Sabbath-breaking, and so on." Then something happened. "All of a sudden," he writes, "I met Moses, carrying in his hand the law of God, and as he looked at me, he seemed to search me through and through with his eyes of fire. He bade me read, "God's Ten Words" - the ten commandments - and as I read them they all seemed to join in accusing and condemning me in the sight of the thrice-holy Jehovah." Spurgeon had come to realise that he was a sinner in the sight of God and that no amount of "respectability" could save him. He passed through a time of distress and anguish. He tried to earn his peace with God by his own efforts. "Before I came to Christ, I said to myself, 'It surely cannot be that, if I believe in Jesus, just as I am, I shall be saved? I must feel something; I must do something.'" But it did not work. His efforts brought him no peace. "They were good for nothing - poor stuff to build eternal hopes upon. Oh, that working for salvation! What slavery it was ...!"

The first Sabbath of the New Year after Spurgeon's return from Newmarket, 6th January, 1850, dawned cold and snowing heavily. Unable to attend church some nine miles away, he turned into an obscure street and saw there a little church building. It was Artillery Street Primitive Methodist Chapel in Colchester. Spurgeon, then a little over fifteen years of age, entered.

The minister did not come that morning, probably because of the snow storm. Spurgeon describes what happened: "At last a very thin looking man, a shoemaker, or tailor, or something of that sort, went up into the pulpit to preach. Now it is well that preachers should be instructed, but this man was really stupid. He was obliged to stick to his text, for the simple reason that he had little else to say. The text was, "Look unto Me, and be ye saved, all the ends of the earth." Spurgeon continues: "He did not even pronounce the words rightly, but that did not matter There was, I thought, a glimpse of hope for me in that text." The good, but ill-equipped man struggled along with his text. Spurgeon remembered it vividly. "Look unto Me, Ay!" said he, in broad Essex, "many on ye are looking' to yourselves, but it's no use lookin' there. You'll not never find comfort in yourselves." Over and over he repeated the words, "Look unto *Me!*" Eventually he came to the end of his tether. Then something remarkable happened. The preacher fixed his eyes on Spurgeon, seated under the gallery. "Young man," he said, "you look very miserable, and you always will be miserable - miserable in life and miserable in death - if you don't obey my text; but if you obey now, this moment, you will be saved." "Then," writes Spurgeon, "lifting up his hands, he shouted, as only a Primitive Methodist could do, 'Young man, look to Jesus Christ. Look! Look! Look! You have nothing to do but to look and live.'" Spurgeon looked. He says, "I could have leaped, I could have danced; there was no expression, however fanatical, which would have been out of keeping with the joy of my spirit at that hour .. I thought I could have sprung from my seat on which I sat, and have called out with the wildest of those Methodist brethren who were present, 'I am forgiven! I am forgiven! A monument of grace! A sinner saved by blood!' My spirit saw its chains broken to pieces; I felt that it was an emancipated soul, an heir of heaven, a forgiven one, accepted in Jesus Christ, plucked out of the miry clay and out of the horrible pit, with my feet set upon a rock, and my goings established. I thought I could dance all the way home."

No fewer than three persons later claimed to have been the preacher that morning, but Spurgeon did not recognise any of them as the man who had pointed him so dramatically to Christ.

Spurgeon's first literary effort was an essay entitled, "Antichrist and Her Brood," in competition for a prize for an essay on Popery. No prize was awarded, but he did receive a handsome gift from a certain Samuel Morely as an encouragement. At the age of sixteen he preached his first sermon from I Peter 2: 7, at the village of Teversham, some four miles from Cambridge. He had commenced his life's work, preaching and writing the gospel. In addition he was to manage an orphanage and a college for the training of pastors. He died on 31st January, 1892. The news of the passing of this man of God was flashed around the world and everywhere the Lord's people, regardless of denomination, felt a sense of unspeakable loss. Among the first of hundreds of messages of sympathy sent to Mrs. Spurgeon, was one from the Prince and Princess of Wales. Eternity alone will reveal how many have been led to know the Lord through the spoken and written ministry of Charles Haddon Spurgeon.

THOMAS BARNARDO

❖

Thomas John Barnardo was born in Dublin on 4th July, 1845. His father, John Michaells Barnardo, a German Jew, became a naturalized British subject when the family banking business in Hamburg, which had helped finance Napoleon, collapsed after the battle of Waterloo. John Barnardo came to Dublin about 1823 and set up business in Dame Street as a furrier. He also made a great deal of money by speculating in stocks and shares. His first wife Elizabeth O'Brien, died giving birth to her sixth child. In due course John married her sister, Abigail O'Brien, legal difficulties being overcome by having the marriage performed in a German church in London and by a German pastor.

Thomas Barnardo was his father's tenth child. The day of his birth was not a happy one for his father, for on that same day the Wicklow-Wexford Railway Company went bankrupt and Mr Barnardo, who held shares in the company, lost several thousand pounds. To make matters worse, the doctor told him that the new baby was delicate and might not live more than a few days. Thomas did survive, but was delicate, hard to rear and experienced several critical illnesses in his early years. Indeed, at the age of two he was pronounced dead and when the undertakers lifted the small body from the bed, the movement caused his heart to flutter and he was found to be alive after all!

Thomas was a difficult child. He was often ill, yet high-spirited and quick tempered. Some of the less pleasant traits discernible in his youth persisted through his life and terms like flamboyant, arrogant and autocratic have all been applied to him with some measure of justification. He was sent to the famous St Patrick's Cathedral Grammar School, but disliked study and this dislike was increased by the brutal conduct of one of the masters and the toleration of a great deal of bullying. With a great sense of relief Barnardo left school at the age of sixteen and entered business, gaining experience in management which was to prove invaluable in later years.

The revival of 1859 in Ulster was beginning to affect many parts of Ireland. Barnardo's mother, Abigail, like her sister Elizabeth, had been brought up in a Protestant faith, although their mother had married into a Roman Catholic family. Abigail was influenced by the Revival and her son. Thomas, was soon to be challenged by the gospel of Christ. Although a confirmed member of the established Church, Thomas found attractive the ideas of the french rationalists, Voltaire and Rousseau.

In the spring of 1862, evangelistic meetings were being held in the Metropolitan Hall in Abbey Street (many such meetings were being held in various parts of the city at that time), and as one of his biographers, Lady Gillian Wagner, puts it,

"Tom Barnardo reluctantly allowed himself to be taken to some of these meetings." For some time he remained unmoved, having no sense of personal need and every confidence in his ability to manage his own life. It was in the home of William Fry, who built Merrion Hall for the Brethren movement in Dublin, that Barnardo first began to doubt his way of life.

There are several accounts of the events that led to Barnardo's conversion, including the preaching of a converted actor John Hambleton. Probably different influences were at work in his life more or less simultaneously. A letter written by Barnardo in 1903 to Mr Lavington Dixon contains his own account of his experience of grace. He writes: "I was brought to Christ in the year 1862. A gentleman, a personal friend of mine, a Dr Hunt of Harcourt Street, Dublin ... had been the means in God's hands of awakening inquiry in the mind of my brother George, who was then at Trinity, of my brother Fred, who was at the school of medicine ... and of myself a little later on." He goes on to tell that his brother Fred's conversion was a great help to him, but concludes, "I actually found Christ without human intervention." He was alone with God when the great change took place.

The change was immediately apparent. He discarded the works of Voltaire and Rousseau and turned, instead, to the Bible. The Brethren movement was then well established in Dublin and was, to some extent, a protest against the dead formalism in many churches. Barnardo found his spiritual home among the Brethren and immediately desired to express his new-found faith in a practical way. In the early days of his Christian life he was influenced by such men as George Muller, Dr. Grattan Guinness and Hudson Taylor. On hearing Taylor, Barnardo volunteered to go to China as a medical missionary. His father, who had hoped to have him in the family business, was strongly opposed to this decision and refused him any financial assistance. But with the help of some friends in Merrion Hall, he was able to go to London in 1866.

One of the things that impressed Barnardo in London was the number of ragged, homeless children. Gradually his interests and energy were channelled towards ministering to these neglected waifs. With the encouragement of Lord Shaftesbury, he organised "ragged schools" found accommodation for waifs and strays and finally opened his first home for boys - a rented house. He refused to run into debt and was firm on this point until one night out of six needy boys he accepted five and sadly refused the sixth, a red-haired lad known as "Carrots". The other boys implored Barnardo to give the boy shelter, but all in vain. Barnardo stood by his principles. A few days later "Carrots" was found dead, the victim of starvation and exposure. Then Barnardo erected a large notice outside his Stepney home: "No destitute boy or girl is ever refused aid." From that hour he trusted God to meet his need. He was never disappointed.

In 1873 Barnardo married Miss Syrie Elmslie, who was also interested in caring for unwanted and unloved children - the ultimate in human sadness! She shared his Christian convictions and it was she who helped him open homes for girl waifs. Barnardo literally worked himself to death. He died in September 1905, shortly after his sixtieth birthday, as the result of the last of a series of heart attacks. From 1867 until his death, he had opened 112 district "Homes" for waifs and strays, and saved almost 60,000 children from destitution and worse! "Encyclopaedia Briticannica" records that of the many thousands sent to Canada by Barnardo's emigration system, less than two percent proved failures! Given the background of the young people concerned, this is an astounding result and shows the worth of evangelical philanthropy. It was Christian compassion that moved people like Elizabeth Fry, Lord Shaftesbury, Florence Nightingale, Thomas Barnardo and many more to recognise and accept their social responsibility in a needy world. To such people faith was never without works. When Thomas Barnardo's "tired and overworked heart ceased to beat," to quote form Norman Wymer's sketch of his life, "thousands of children lost a friend to whom they owed everything." Many of those children, however, had found another Friend through the witness of Barnardo and his Homes - "a Friend that sticketh closer than a brother."

SAMUEL BILL

❖

The name of Samuel Alexander Bill may no longer be the household word it once was in Christian circles in Ulster, but the Mission which he founded, the Qua Iboe Mission, is still widely supported. Samuel Bill was born on the outskirts of Belfast in January 1864 and, like another Samuel, was dedicated to God by his parents before he was born. He was a kind and affectionate boy. He once won a cash prize at school and he changed the silver coins into copper (to look bigger!) and brought them home as a present for his mother. His father was a builder and when Samuel left school he was apprenticed to the trade. His close friend in those days, and indeed, throughout life, was Archie Bailie. They liked to call each other "Jonathan" and "David"; it was that kind of friendship.

Samuel and Archie loved to go for strolls on summer evenings and on star-lit nights they studied astronomy.

Another past-time which they enjoyed was swimming in the Connswater where it flowed into the sea. It was here that Samuel surprised his instructor by proposing to swim the full breadth of the estuary, a feat only attempted by experienced swimmers. He not only succeeded in reaching the other side, but turned and swam back again! It was this kind of courage and resolution which characterised him in future years as a pioneer missionary. Quite unknown to Samuel, God was preparing him for a tough and dangerous field of service.

Samuel Bill faithfully attended Ballymacarret Presbyterian Church and was always present in the Bible Class, where the Rev. Dr. John Maneely instructed the members in the truths of God's Word. Yet, like that other Samuel, he "did not yet know the Lord, neither was the word of the Lord revealed unto him." Eva Stuart Watt comments that he "was just taking life as he found it, working hard during the week, going to Church and Bible Class ... but every Saturday coming into the city to buy himself the latest novel."

His Sabbath School teacher, Bob McCall, had led him as a lad to the Saviour. When the evangelists Moody and Sankey came to Belfast in the late "Seventies," Samuel was about 18 years of age. He and his friend Archie attended the meetings and Samuel's commitment to Christ was confirmed and his consecration became more marked. At that time many young men and women were brought to know the Lord, and there was widespread evangelistic activity. One group of Christian workers consisted of Samuel Bill, Archie Bailie and John McKittrick, who witnessed in an old schoolroom in Club Row. Along with some others they helped to establish the Mountpottinger branch of the Y.M.C.A. There, every Saturday night, Samuel and Archie met for prayer and to seek God's guidance for future service.

Samuel Bill attended a series of lectures in his church, given by Rev. Dr. William Rodgers, of Whiteabbey, entitled "Glimpses at the Map of the World." Dr. Rodgers sought to stimulate missionary interest by indicating a number of needy fields where there were no missionaries. Samuel now knew where his duty lay.

With reference to missionary work, the comment has been made, "No man needs a call when he has already been given a command! What he does need is guidance as to how to obey." To some that may seem an over-simplification, yet it contains an element of truth which has been too often forgotten. Those young men in Belfast - Bill, Bailie and McKittrick - were fully aware of their missionary obligations; what they sought was guidance and opportunity.

John McKittrick entered Harley College in London, where Dr. Grattan Guinness was Principal. He became the pioneer of the Congo-Balolo Mission in West Africa, where he was overcome by the climate and died after five years' work. Soon after McKittrick went to Harley, Samuel Bill followed and Archie Bailie came a year later.

The door of opportunity opened for Samuel quite unexpectedly. For some time members of the Ibuno tribe visiting Calabar for purposes of trade had been in touch with Christians at Duketown and a white trader had been holding regular "God palavers" with chiefs near the mouth of the Qua Iboe river. Thus a desire for further knowledge was born and the chiefs' request for a missionary was sent to Dr. Grattan Guinness at Harley College. At the breakfast table Dr. Guinness read the letter slowly, rose to his feet and informed the students of its contents. "It's a wild country and a treacherous climate," he said, "but will any of you young men volunteer to go?" After prayerful consideration, it was Samuel Bill who said "I will." His friend, Archie, was to follow him later.

In due course Samuel Bill was ready to sail for Qua Iboe. He was to be supported at home by a small but devoted band of praying and giving Christians, with names like Morrison, Ferguson, McMaster and Steele. On the eve of his embarkation he surprised Dr. Guinness with a letter saying that he had cancelled his passage and was postponing departure until the next boat, because he had "just found his Rebecca"! This proved to be a young English girl, Gracie Kerr, whom he met in a friend's house. It was love at first sight. Gracie shared Samuel's vision and entered Doric Lodge, the girl's missionary school connected with Harley College. Samuel returned for his bride when her training was complete. They were married on October 14, 1890, in Mountpottinger Presbyterian Church, Belfast.

Gracie was often ill and sometimes had to return to Ireland, but even then she laboured for Christ's cause in Qua Iboe and was instrumental in moving others to go there. The story of the early days of this Mission in an area so unhealthy as to be called "the white man's grave" and amid dangerous tribes, is thrilling to read. Never has greater bravery been displayed by missionaries; but they thought only in terms of love and compassion. Samuel Bill died on 24th January, 1942. At that time there were fifteen Central Stations with seven hundred and fifty out-stations in charge of about seven hundred teachers and evangelists and a total membership of over fifty thousand. Today the Qua Iboe church has 990 churches, 88,000 communicant members, 105 pastors and 770 preachers.

Samuel Bill was honoured by the King when the M.B.E. was conferred on him. There is no doubt that he received a higher reward from the King of kings. This man went out ALONE; but he was not alone, for GOD was with him. Selah (Think about that!)

AMY CARMICHAEL

❖

Amy Beatrice Carmichael was born on 16th December, 1867, in the coastal village of Millisle in County Down, Northern Ireland. Her name is recorded in the baptismal register of the Presbyterian Church at Ballycopeland and the date is January 19th, 1868. At that time most of the men in Millisle were employed by the Carmichael Flour Mills which had been in the family for over a hundred years. For several generations the Carmichaels had been a god-fearing people. The family was of Covenanting stock and came from Ayrshire in Scotland.

Amy Carmichael's great-grandfather, Robert, was forty yeas of age when a Presbyterian Church was built on the edge of the seashore at Ballycopeland. The Presbyterians who built this church belonged to a group known as the "Anti-Burgher Seceders," who left the Church of Scotland in the early eighteenth century on conscientious grounds relating to purity of doctrine and patronage rights. Years later, after the Carmichael family had left the district, the congregation joined with the non-seceding Presbyterians at Millisle and the Ballycopeland church building fell into disuse. Its ruins, almost washed by the waves, may still be seen.

Amy's father, David Carmichael, did not marry until he was in his thirty-seventh years, and he made a wise choice. His wife's name was Catherine Jane Filson, a doctor's daughter from Portaferry on Strangford Lough. Like her husband, Catherine had been brought up in a godly home and had seen something of the revival of 1859. Amy was the eldest of seven children and they were all instructed in the Scriptures and the Shorter Catechism.

Amy grew up a gentle, kind girl. She was especially kind to the sick and needy. Her childhood days in Millisle were very happy. Competition with American flour mills brought the first great change in Amy's life. The Carmichaels moved to Belfast and built a new mill near the Dufferin Dock and they took up residence in College Gardens. Before that, Amy had spent three years at a Wesleyan Methodist boarding school at Harrowgate, Yorkshire, where she earned the dual reputation of being a rather wild Irish girl who was also very kind! She was probably irked by the many petty rules of this establishment.

It was near the end of her stay at Harrowgate, about 1883, that Amy was converted. She attended a mission held by the C.S.S.M. Although she knew the way of salvation very well, she had never really committed herself to Christ and thus obeyed the gospel. During this mission she realised that she must come to Christ and this she did. Shortly afterwards she found much satisfaction in the well known lines:

Upon a life I did not live,
Upon a death I did not die,
Another's life, Another's death,
I stake my whole eternity.

Back in Belfast, Amy soon became compassionately involved with the poor and underprivileged mill workers of the city. Henry Montgomery of the Belfast City Mission used to take her on Saturday evenings through the poorer streets of Belfast and the sights of poverty and evil made a deep impression on Amy's mind and heart. Soon she was engaged in helping the "shawlies" or mill girls and shocked many respectable church goers in so doing. One minister's wife remarked indignantly, "I would let no child of mine go down those streets." Amy commented, "Perhaps my mother believed in an angel guard."

While staying at Broughton Grange in the Lake District, the home of Robert Wilson, a leading member of the Society of Friends, God laid on her heart a burden which turned her thoughts to missionary work. In a letter to her mother she wrote, "I heard Him say, 'Go ye.' I never heard it just so plainly before; I cannot be mistaken, for I know, He spoke. He says 'Go'. I cannot stay." Her mother replied, "Amy ... you are His - to take you where He pleases and to use you as He pleases. I can trust you to Him, and I do - and I thank Him for letting you hear His voice as you have done ... 'Go ye' - my heart echoes."

Amy was soon to discover that missionary doors that seem to be ajar can be very stiff on their hinges! For a while she pushed hard on such stubborn doors. Eventually she was allowed to sail with three women missionaries of the China Inland Mission to Shanghai, where she received word that C.M.S. Missionaries would make her welcome in Japan. There she laboured for about a year. She was to find her life's work not in Japan, but in India where she became the missionary to the temple children who were intended for a life of darkness and shame. Her heart bled for them and soon her great work of rescuing these perishing ones began. At first, when Amy heard of the terrible plight of these children, she said to herself, "Something must be done about it." Soon she found the burden of concern so heavy that she said "I must do something about it." She did. The famous Home at Dohnavur was founded and later the Dohnavur Fellowship in South India was established. Through the loving labours of Amy Carmichael, hundreds of children were *saved*, in every sense of that great word. Any was no doctrinaire missiologist obsessed with academic considerations. Her burden for the lost was too great to permit her such intellectual luxuries. In the spirit of the One Who came to seek and to save the lost, she gave her life unhesitatingly and unstintingly in His great service. It is not surprising, then, that her devotional writings are gems of wisdom, experience and reflection. They include "Edges of His Ways," "Gold by Moonlight" and "Windows." Stories of Indian women including "Mimosa" and "Kohila". Her poetic nature constantly expressed itself in delightful verse. There is a certain rebuke in her lines:

> Many crowd the Saviour's Kingdom;
> Few receive His cross.
> Many see His consolation;
> Few will suffer loss.

The dominant role in Amy's poetry is that of sweet, precious fellowship with her Saviour, the real secret of her wonderful life of service to others. She wrote:

Lord, give me love, then I have all,
For love casts out tormenting fear,
And love sounds forth a trumpet call
To valiant hope, and sweet and clear
The birds of joy sing in my tree,
Love of my heart, when I have Thee.

Amy, this lovely, Christ-like lady, slipped quietly Home on 18th January, 1951, after fifty-nine years of missionary service.

ISOBEL KUHN

❖

Isobel Miller was born on 17th December, 1901, in the home of her maternal grandmother, Octavia Selina Irish (she was Irish!) at 60 Henry Street, Toronto, Canada. Her parents were Samuel and Alice Miller. Her father's work involved much travel and Isobel, in her youth, saw such cities as Pittsburgh, Cleveland, Philadelphia and St. Louis. There was nothing particularly dramatic about her childhood, unless we note that she nearly died when just one week old. Her brother Murray, who was then two-and-a-half years old, decided to carry his sister downstairs to her mother and finding her too heavy, left her hanging head down! When discovered she was blue in the face and scarcely breathing! Mercifully the tiny heart was restored to its normal rhythm.

Isobel's grandfather was a Presbyterian minister and her father frequently conducted services of worship. As a girl she

was well instructed in the Christian Faith and buttressed against
the attacks on that Faith by modernism. She benefited from
the Christian atmosphere of her home, although her father's
preference for Isobel and her mother's preference for Murray
did give rise to a certain amount of friction.

On entering high school, Isobel won the Governor-
General's medal for all British Columbia. Later, while studying in the University of British Columbia, Vancouver, Isobel's
intellectual acceptance of Christianity was put to the test. In
the English class the Professor was discussing the Bible. "Of
course," he said, "no one in this enlightened age believes any
more in the myths of Genesis and ..." He paused and said, "Is
there any one here who believes ... that the story of Genesis is
true? Please raise your hand." Isobel mustered enough courage to raise her hand and as she looked around the classroom,
she saw that just one other hand was raised. The Professor
smiled and told them that they just believed this because their
parents had told them so. Isobel could have taken an
argument, but not a sneer. The incident shook her acceptance
of the Biblical record and she decided to keep an "open mind"
and endeavour to be scientific in her attitude to the Bible and
religion. This was an altogether new stance for Isobel. In reality her "open mind" meant setting on the side the instruction
received in her home.

Then another shadow fell across this young life. For some
time she had given her affection to a tall young student called
Ben and was engaged to marry him. One day a college chum
felt compelled to tell Isobel that Ben was going out with another girl behind her back. Isobel was stunned. The ensuring
confrontation with Ben led to the ending of their relationship
and Isobel was dazed and broken-hearted by the experience.
She had no Christian conviction to sustain her. Once, when
her father knelt by her bedside and prayed for her, she

commented, "Thanks, Dad, I know you mean it well, but it doesn't go beyond the ceiling, you know." He turned with a groan and left the room.

Isobel's misery reached its climax on the eve of her twentieth birthday. The Post Office clock had just struck 2 a.m. and the tense, desperate girl lay awake in hopeless despair. The tempter's voice was clear and persistent: "Of what use is life?" She remembered that bottle in the bathroom marked "Poison". The terrible idea which had entered her mind seemed the only solution to her problems. She rose to make her way to the bathroom. As she turned the door knob, she heard her father moaning in his sleep. Three times she heard him. She loved him and she thought to herself that if she committed suicide, he would break his heart, thinking she had gone to hell. She could not do that to him. "In agony," she writes, "I turned and sat down on the edge of my bed and faced the darkest moment of my life. I didn't want to live and I couldn't die." It was then that she remembered a line of poetry: "In His will is our peace." A battle was raging in her heart. What if there were a God, after all? If so, her life had not been pleasing to Him. Maybe that was why she had no peace. Suddenly she raised her hands and whispered in the darkness, "God, if there be a God, if you will prove to me that You are, and if You will give me peace, I will give you my whole life. I'll do anything You ask me to do, go where You send me, obey You all my days." Ah! what anguish was in that cry of the heart. The Professor who sowed the seed of doubt in Isobel's mind, was the cause of so much of her distress, and yet, in the providence of God, he was used to topple mere intellectual acceptance of Christianity and so prepare the way for her conversion. God makes the wrath of man to praise Him (Ps. 76:10).

Isobel lay down and did what she had mostly failed to do, fell asleep. It was sound, healthy sleep, like that of a little child. When she awoke, she remembered her prayer and her promise. She had prayed for peace and peace had come. Was not that the hand of God? So why not keep her promise? Isobel was now seeking the Lord. Her parents were unaware of this, but they sensed that she was changed. One day her mother begged her to come to hear a Professor Ellis who was giving lectures in Vancouver Bible School. Isobel went and for the first time heard a conservative scholar. He was radiant with Christian love and joy. As she listened, her mind and heart alike were satisfied. Ellis answered the sceptics, but did so without a trace of abuse or sarcasm. Isobel was impressed and she returned many times to hear this man of God expound the Scriptures. As she listened, her experience was similar to Lydia of old. The Lord opened her heart (Acts 16:14).

Isobel graduated in May, 1922. When she sensed a call to missionary service, she entered the Moody Bible Institute in Chicago. There she met and immediately fell in love with a Dutchman named John Kuhn (she had made up her mind not to have any boy-friends at Moody!). She married John on 4th November, 1929. In her books, "By Searching," and "Into the Arena" Isobel Kuhn tells her amazing story. She and her husband spent twenty years working among the Lisu tribe in south-west China, and with the China Inland Mission (now the Overseas Missionary Fellowship).

Because of Communist occupation in 1950, they were forced to leave. In Thailand they continued to work among the Lisu people.

In 1954 Isobel came home for surgery. As the result of an accident she had developed cancer. She died on 20th March, 1957. Her husband was alone with her. It was a solemn, precious moment - their last earthly moment together. "If I was ever near heaven," he said, "and I was ever conscious that death has lost its sting, it was then." Near the end of her life

Isobel wrote to her brother, "I am trusting only in Christ's merits for salvation; my own life has been too full of faults and failures to be worth anything ... I am so grateful He led me to Himself when I was young so that I could have this long earthly walk with Him. I recommend Him as a peerless Master." Reader, pay heed to her words.

GLADYS AYLWARD

❖

Gladys May Aylward was born in Edmonton, North London, on 24th February, 1902. Her mother's name was Whiskin and she is described by one biographer as "a thorough-going little Cockney with her ready wit and her love for bright colours and plenty of feathers in her hat, when hats had feathers in them." Gladys certainly inherited her mother's bright and plucky nature.

At the age of fourteen Gladys found a job as an assistant in the Penny Bazaar, where nothing on sale cost more than a penny! Later she went to serve in a grocer's shop, but when men began to return from the First World War wanting their jobs back, Gladys had to find employment as a parlourmaid in the West End. Hours were long and pay was small, but Gladys enjoyed life in the heart of the great city. She found it all exciting. She was particularly fond of the theatre. For a few pence she could obtain a cheap seat and she dreamed of being an actress herself. The theatre fired her imagination - an imagination that often ran riot!

One Tuesday evening as she strolled aimlessly along, she was spotted by a group of young people standing near a church. They invited her to come inside and, linking arms, led her inside the building. She was rather annoyed by this and listened to the service with some resentment. She had heard it all before. At the close she was making a hasty retreat, when someone at the door grasped her hand, asked her name and said, "Miss Aylward, I believe God is wanting you." That really frightened her and she left at once. This proved to be a disturbing experience which she was unable to forget. Eventually she went to see a Rev. F.W. Pitt. He was not at home, but his kindly wife invited her in and talked to her. She told Gladys the way of salvation. Gladys knew it all. Quietly the minister's wife insisted that Gladys could not be neutral where Christ was concerned and urged her to obey the gospel and trust in Christ as her Saviour. Nothing dramatic happened. It was all so unlike the theatre. But she knelt down beside the good lady and prayed for forgiveness, committing herself to Christ for ever. She stood up a different person. Now she knew that she belonged to Christ and that He was her Lord.

Soon Gladys began talking about China. She wanted to be a missionary. At first no one took her seriously, but Gladys persisted. Her father tried to dissuade her. "Are you a nurse?" "No." "Are you a teacher?" "No." "Then what good do you think you'd do going to China?" Her father was angry. "Talk about going to China! talk, talk! That's all you an do - just talk!" Gladys crept out of the room and stood crying at the foot of the stairs. Suddenly she stopped crying and whispered, "Talk - talk *but that's it!*" Now she really was going to talk - to the right people in the right places!

She stood before the headquarters of the China Inland Mission, and above the doorway she read the words, "Have Faith in God"! The C.I.M. decided that Gladys be sent to a Training Home to study. When it came to lecture time she was lost! Finally the chairman of the committee interviewed her and told her as kindly as possible that he believed that God had a plan for her life, possibly in England, but not as a missionary overseas. Gladys was stunned. She had been turned down, and she had been so sure that she was going to China and that God was calling her to go there. Now she could not see the way ahead. Everything at that moment seemed dark.

It was suggested to Gladys that she might like to help two missionaries home on furlough. So she went to Bristol and there the missionaries told her about their experiences. They gave her a little card with the motto, "Be not afraid, remember the Lord." She kept it in her Bible.

The days and months passed and Gladys took a job as Assistant Matron in the Sunshine Hostel in Swansea, where girls were taken in for a night's lodgings. Often Gladys would go looking for these girls in the dockland, where sailors left their ships with money in their pockets and time on their hands. Here Gladys saw the seamy side of life - poverty, filth, degradation. She was appalled. She was burdened by what she saw and some told her that *this* was her mission field. Why go thousands of miles away to China, when there was so much to do here at home? But God had written China on Gladys heart, and no power, or logic or wisdom on earth could erase it.

Finally there came that day when Gladys was almost thirty. She was back in London, sitting in her bedroom. Beside her was her Bible and Daily Light and a few pennies - all the money she possessed in the world. In tears the London parlourmaid knelt, placed her hand on her few coppers and prayed with passionate earnestness, "Oh God, here's me. Here's

my Bible, here's my money! Use us, God! Use us!" She rose
to hear her name being called. It was one of the other maids to
say that her mistress wished to see her. The mistress had called
her to explain that it was her practice to pay the fares of her
maids when she engaged them. When Gladys returned to her
room she held three shillings in her hand, ten times the amount
she had placed on her Bible when she cried to God! She saw it
as coming straight from God towards her fare to China. If He
could multiply what she gave Him as quickly as that, she would
soon be there! God did the necessary multiplication and He
opened the door as well.

One evening someone said to Gladys, "I've got a friend
who's got a friend who has just gone to China ... She is
seventy-three and has been a missionary in China for years.
She came home, but she couldn't settle, so she's gone out again.
She's praying for some young person to go out and join her
..." "That's me," interrupted Gladys. On Saturday 15th October, 1932, she left Liverpool Street Station en route for China.
Thus began the astonishing missionary saga of "the small
woman," as she was called. (See "A London Sparrow," by
Phyllis Thompson, and "The Small Woman," by Alan
Burgess). The journeyings of this lone woman, her dauntless
courage in the presence of danger during the Sino-Japanese
war, her trek across the mountains with scores of children to
escape the advancing Japanese forces, and much more - all of
this is quite incredible apart from the power of God.

Gladys died early in 1970 after an attack of "flu with
pleurisy". Her name is inscribed for ever in the annals of
missionary enterprise. She was a missionary against all "the
rules of the book," this brave little soul who, despite her lack
of formal training, normally and properly required by mission
boards, was faithful to her call from God and signally used by
Him.

FRED WRIGHT

❖

Sometimes Christian witness in the home is a means in God's hand to lead another member of the family to Himself. This was so in the case of Fred Wright who was to become a twentieth century martyr.

Mr and Mrs William Wright had a family of eight boys and three girls. They worshipped in St. Enoch's and then Duncairns Presbyterian churches in Belfast. The children attended Sabbath School regularly and cheerfully and were trained to be obedient and useful from early years. Mrs Wright had stronger religious inclinations than her husband, an attitude which, by God's grace, was to deepen and grow in future years.

Fred as the sixth child in this happy family. He had a great sense of humour and was a keen athlete, being particularly interested in rugby, swimming and boxing. The late

Mr. Ireland, General Secretary of the Belfast Y.M.C.A. said of him, that he was "the toughest and cleanest player he had ever watched. He feared nothing." A close fried of Fred's, Rev. R. Gordon Williamson, wrote, "He did not know the meaning of fear, and I am convinced that there never was a man more eminently fitted for the work of a pioneer missionary than was Fred Wright."

Fred's brother, Joe, was the first of the family to experience conversion, being led to Christ by Rev. Mr. Nesbit, at that time assistant in Townsend Street Presbyterian church. Joe was then fifteen or sixteen years of age, and it was largely through his influence that Fred came to trust in the Saviour, while still in his teens. Rev. R. Gordon Williamson writes, "I can remember the first forming Fred came into business after his conversion. He was anxious right away to tell everybody about it and soon expressed a desire to do something for Christ, his new-found Master. Together we began to read for the ministry, but about that time Fred's brother Joe, who was already on the Mission Field, was writing to him stories that stirred his imagination. He longed to go out to Amazonia himself, and the call came very definitely."

From the moment of his conversion, Fred was outstanding in his loyalty and devotion to Christ. He was actively involved in the work of his church and in the Y.M.C.A. Mr Ireland, of the Y.M.C.A., retarded Fred as an "out and outer," whether on the rugby field or in his witness for Christ. For him salvation meant, to quote his brother Joe, "a life to be lived, a race to be run, and a fight to be fought." He was a wholesome happy Christian. As Joe Wright puts it, "He was not a pious puke!"

This young man was refreshingly different in so many ways and always fearless. Once, when he discovered that a certain big city firm had dispensed with the services of a poor cleaner, without any recognition of her twenty-five years service, he went straight to the management and expressed himself so forcefully that the woman received a pension for the rest of her life. Mr Joe Wright tells that Fred "used to rush home from the rugby field, and after a clean-up and a meal, would visit some needy mothers and widows, scrub and wash their floors, before going to a Bible Class or Fellowship meeting."

Fred Wright was generous to a fault. He was employed by a linen firm and always he gave his pay packet, unopened, to his mother, and was satisfied with whatever pocket money she gave him. Once the pay packet contained more than usual and he returned the extra cash on Monday, only to discover that he had been given a rise!

In 1934 Fred Wright was to go to Brazil where he met two other Freds - Fred Roberts, an Australian, and Fred Dawson who was born in Tasmania. They were working under the auspices of the Unevangelised Fields Mission. In the providence of God, their missionary target would prove to be hitherto unreached Kayapo Indians of the Xingu forests of Brazil. Mr Horace Banner comments, "No mere human selection had called together these comrades with one common name, 'Fred'. This was God's planning." They were to prove a fearless, united missionary band.

The break with home had not been easy for the Irish Fred. There was strong opposition from his firm. Joe Wright tells what happened. "Fred ... knew the linen business from the seed up. The firm wanted to send him to the continent. In fact he had been taking lessons in Spanish for that purpose. His resignation was a bombshell. All the manager's arguments were in vain. Finally he sent for his father and sought his help to dissuade Fred from such a mad adventure, pointing out the glorious prospects of the firm's offer ... Father, too, became angry with Fred and strongly opposed him. The manager's last words to Fred as he turned to go were, 'Wright, you're a damned fool'!"

Fred Wright trained at the Missionary Training colony in Upper Norwood, London, where he enlivened the scene with his many escapades and endless wit. But one day a friend found him sitting with bowed head and with tears in his eyes. He asked the reason. Quietly Fred put into his hand a tiny package which he had just received in the post. It contained a returned engagement ring. Then Fred stood up, wiped his eyes and said bravely, "I'm going through with God," and slowly walked away.

On the mission field, Fred Wright showed all the qualities he had displayed at home - thoughtfulness, kindness, humour, generosity, fearlessness and utter selflessness. His brother Joe, then deputy Field Leader, was deeply impressed by Fred's devotion to his Lord. "And," he says, "there never was any sanctimonious or pious patter."

In 1935 the three Freds reached the Kayapo Indians and were never seen again. Later a search party found the remains of their motor boat and some other items that seemed to indicate a violent end to their quest. Back in Ulster, Fred Wright's mother, on hearing the news, knelt and prayed, "Father, forgive them, for they know not what they do."

One night, at a Missionary Prayer Meeting in Bangor, Fred Wright had prayed with great earnestness, "Oh Lord, if it please Thee, let me go as a missionary, and, yes, let me die as a martyr for Thee."

God granted his prayer in full.

In his last letter to his prayer-partners, Fred Wright wrote: "Once we leave civilisation, it may be months or even years before we can come down with mail. It may be that we shall never get down again; God only knows. As far as we can ascertain, the Kayapos are very numerous. We are quite aware that, humanly speaking, we are as good as dead men; but, brethren, stand by us as one man. Do not criticise. We are beyond criticism as we go forward in the Name of the Lord and under His command after having fully counted the cost. Finally, it is well to remember that Calvary was and is the greatest victory of all times. Death to the Christian is not defeat. Should the Lord will that we be taken, our prayer is that more men and more money be rushed out to follow this advance ..."

That prayer was answered. The U.F.M. did follow up the advance. Fred's mother knelt in prayer and claimed one hundred Kayapos for each Fred slain, and today there are over three hundred Kayapos in the fold of the Good Shepherd. "Some" says Joe Wright, "are pastors, some evangelists, others teachers. Some were employed on the Trans-Amazon Highway, a mammoth four thousand mile project. The Brazilian engineers working on that project were awed one day to find a group of Kayapos meeting for prayer at break time and giving thanks to God for their meagre meal. One young Kayapo Indian lad is a pilot in the Brazilian Air Force. Is not God sovereign?" Who could have foreseen what the conversion of this Belfast lad would mean for the Kingdom of God?

In 1964, Rev. Joe Wright and his wife were flown in to the area at Smoke Falls where the massacre had occurred. Using Fred's own Brazilian Bible, which was found in his trunk, Joe witnessed to the Kayapos. When he finished, a tall Kayapo stood up and spoke. This is how Joe Wright records the incident. "'Who is this man?' All eyes turned on me. Silence! 'He is actually a brother of one of the three we killed. Why has he come? To take vengeance? No; this man has come to speak of love, pardon and forgiveness.' Then, with outstretched arms, he made a passionate plea for his own people to become 'Jesus hearers,' an Indian expression normally used for hearing and fearing the spirit world.'

As Joe Wright listened, he knew that Fred did not die in vain. He noticed the little swellings on the tall Indian's chest and back - his name was Turtle Dove! He had been the greatest and cruelest killer of the tribe, for each swelling represented a killing. The swellings were the result of a knife incision filled with charred leaves.

Eventually the story of the massacre was pieced together. The missionaries had been received with apparent friendliness. Presents had been accepted. Later the Indians managed to separate the Freds and killed them one by one. None of the missionaries knew what had happened to the others. One day an Indian took Joe Wright to a clump of trees at the edge of the river and indicated the spot where his brother Fred had been clubbed to death. That night, with two hurricane lamps tied to a tree, the Indians squatting on the ground, Joe again using Fred's Bible, led in worship. At the close of the service, Horace Banner stepped across and said, "Joe there is nothing marking the spot, but look up!" Joe was familiar with that marvellous tropical sky, but he looked up and immediately he knew what Horace Banner meant; for there, directly above, shone the constellation of stars known as the Southern Cross. "Heaven," he thought, "had marked the spot."

We have told the story of one of the Freds. They were all outstanding men of God. While others theorised and debated, they "hazarded their lives for the name of our Lord Jesus Christ" (Acts 15:26). They shared the vision of men like Robert Moffat who wrote:

My album is the savage beast,
Where tempests brood and shadows rest,
Without one ray of light;
To write the name of Jesus there,
To see that savage bow in prayer,
And point to worlds more bright and fair,
This is my soul's delight.

This is one of the greatest missionary sagas of all time. The conversion of such men was not by chance, nor was their early training in life, such as Fred Wright's learning of Spanish. It was all part of God's sovereign plan and to Him alone be the glory.

HELEN ROSEVEARE

❖

Helen Roseveare was born at Haileybury, Hertfordshire, England in 1925. She was a graduate of Newham College, Cambridge, where she studied medicine. It was there that she met Christian students whose quality of life impressed her. She also discovered another side to life as a medical student. On Wednesday mornings a group of students took it in turns to act as "guinea pig" while others administered treatment and took notes. When Helen's turn came she was made to drink gin allegedly to study its effects on the human constitution! Forced to drink more and more she soon became so drunk that she had to be carried through the streets of Cambridge and deposited at the front door of Newham Ladies' College. An understanding and perceptive Principal took no action.

In her earlier school days, Helen had thought about God and when on occasion she misbehaved she felt guilt-stricken.

As she grew older her thoughts became more serious. There were the horrors of the second World War, the hungry and homeless - and few seemed to care. Her religious training was Anglo-Catholic. She longed for a fuller and clearer knowledge of God. "I tried earnestly to help others, to be kindly, to be sincere. I was an ardent Anglo-Catholic, regular at the confessional and the mass, every part of me stretching out after the Unseen Power who could meet all needs". But nothing was happening. She felt increasingly hopeless. "Whilst *in* church, I could lose myself to all the problems, bathed in strange mysticism and pious ritualism; but on leaving the service, I had nothing, no power, no compassion, no help to answer the daily needs and meet the daily problems".

As a result of friendships made at Newham, Helen began to attend the Christian Union Bible studies and prayer meetings, although still a practising Anglo-Catholic. When Christmas came during her first year at Cambridge, she went with some of her friends to a Christian house-party at Mount Hermon Bible College, Ealing. She writes, "I just didn't fit: I didn't talk their language, I couldn't understand their spiritual jargon - but I could understand their happiness and friendliness".

The Bible studies focused on the book of Genesis and the Epistle to the Romans. It was as she studied Romans that the light began to dawn in her soul. "The truth began to penetrate my thick skull - it was true! It was no myth. It was no out-dated fairy-tale. This God was *real*, and true, and vital. He cared ... he loved me enough to die for me ..." It was the moment of decision for Helen. She writes, "I knew with an unshakable assurance that God was real, that His salvation was true, that I was accepted by Him into His family and His service."

Some eight years after entering University, Dr. Helen Roseveare, aged twenty-eight and with a degree in general medicine and surgery, was on her way as a medical missionary to the Belgian Congo under the auspices of the Worldwide Evangelisation Crusade (WEC) - that was in 1953. She never imagined that her task in establishing Christian hospitals would be easy, nor did she dream of how great some of her problems would be. In her books "Give Me This Mountain" and "He Gave Us A Valley" she tells much about her experiences and of the trials she endured in the Master's service.

Her worst and most dangerous experiences were during the Simba uprising and civil war that convulsed the newly formed Republic of Congo. It was then that she was brutally raped, as were other missionaries, the young black male student nurse who tried to save her being savagely beaten to death by the rebel soldiers. That was followed by five months' captivity. Later she was rescued by the National Army and given a year's furlough.

Dr. Roseveare returned to Congo/Zaire and gave seven years' devoted service at the Evangelical Medical Centre of Nyankunde in N.E. Zaire. She returned home in 1973 after twenty years' missionary service - but never retired from the Lord's service, remaining a true missionary of the Cross wherever she went.

How did this devoted missionary view her many arduous years of service? She tells us: "I suddenly knew with every fibre of my being that these twenty years *had* been worthwhile, very, very worthwhile, utterly worthwhile, with no room left for regrets or recriminations." Wherever and however the Lord calls us to serve Him, it is always well worth it - whatever the cost.

W. P. NICHOLSON

❖

William Patteson Nicholson was born in Bangor, County Down, on 3rd April 1876. He was one of a family of seven - the eldest, Sarah, became a missionary with the Irish Presbyterian Mission in Manchuria, and one of his brothers, James, served as a medical missionary in the South Sea Islands for fifteen years.

W.P. Nicholson had a Presbyterian upbringing and he never forgot the faithful evangelical ministry of Rev. Henry Montgomery in Albert Street Church, Belfast, where he had been taken regularly as a boy. He had been taught the Westminster Shorter Catechism at the church school connected with Fisherwick Presbyterian Church.

Nicholson's father, Captain John G. Nicholson, served in the Merchant Navy, and William went to sea at the age of sixteen. For a period he worked with a railway construction gang in South Africa. During those years he lived a godless life and became a slave to strong drink.

His conversion came suddenly and unexpectedly and shows the importance of sound biblical teaching in one's youth. S.W. Murray, in his well documented booklet, "W.P. Nicholson: Flame for God in Ulster", tells how it happened. "After returning home from a spell abroad, he was sitting at his mother's fireside at Bangor on the morning of 22nd May, 1899, awaiting his breakfast, when suddenly he came under deep conviction of sin. A voice spoke within him urging him to repent and believe on Christ. In desperation he made his decision, and, to quote his own words, "Suddenly and powerfully and consciously, I was saved. Such a peace and freedom from fear, such a sweet assurance filled my soul. I turned to my mother and said, 'Mother, I am saved'. She looked at me and nearly collapsed, and said 'When?' I said 'Just now'. 'Where?' 'Here where I am sitting'. She cried with joy unspeakable." It was an answer to the prayers of many years.

Some time after his conversion, Nicholson studied in the Bible Training Institute, Glasgow. Here he was influenced by such notable men as Dr. James Denney, Dr. James Orr and Dr. Alexander Whyte. S.W. Murray comments, "It is not difficult to see the connection between Whyte's fierce self-criticism and analysis of the deceitfulness of sin, and the subsequent fearless denunciation of personal sins and of social evils by the young Irish student."

The early 1920s saw the North of Ireland convulsed by strife and blighted by mass unemployment. Following the partition of Ireland, Ulster experienced a reign of terror and there were numerous atrocities. Fear gripped the hearts of the people as the Province poised on the brink of civil war. It was then that Nicholson returned to Ireland after a time of evangelistic work in Scotland, America and Australia. Intending to

stay for several weeks, he was to remain for six years conduct-
ing missions across the Province - the first of several such
campaigns. During that time in the twenties, thousands were
converted. Wherever he went hundreds came to hear him
preach. The results were astounding. So many examples could
be given. A few must suffice. In 1922 the Shankill Road
Mission Committee reported that in a mission conducted by
Nicholson, some 3,000 people packed the Albert Hall every
evening and 2,260 men, women and young people passed
through the enquiry rooms, most of whom were led to Christ.
At the close of a six week campaign in Londonderry, between
1,300 and 1,400 had passed through the enquiry rooms.

Two missions held in the east end of Belfast were
significant in their impact on the workers in the Queen's
Island shipyard, at that time one of the largest yards in the
world. The results of these missions were astonishing as
hundreds of men were converted and often gun-carrying men
carried Bibles instead.

In 1926 Nicholson was asked at short notice to take part
in a university mission in Cambridge, due to the illness of
Dr. J. Stuart Holden. Some were afraid that because of his
unconventional methods he would prove a misfit. In fact, over
100 undergraduates were converted. The fruit of the Nicholson
campaigns in Ulster was manifold. Scores of men, in all
denominations, felt the call to the Gospel ministry. In just three
years the membership of the Christian Endeavour movement
rose from 5,000 to 10,500. S.W. Murray observes that "while
Nicholson was anything but a college man, his work had a
profound influence on the colleges". It was during this period
that the Bible Union (now the Christian Union) was established
in Queen's University, Belfast. Two medical students were instrumental in this development - both became missionaries,
one in Qua Iboe, Nigeria, the other in Eastern Bengal.

On 15th April, 1914, Nicholson was ordained as an evangelist by the Carlisle Presbytery (Pennsylvania) of the Presbyterian Church in the U.S.A. His methods, however, were far from traditional. Much of his wit and banter in the pulpit, and the resulting laughter, were out of place in a Gospel service. Yet when he began to preach his manner changed. He preached repentance with an awesome solemnity. He dealt faithfully with the sins of the saints, and, despite his unconventional behaviour, God used him mightily and his ministry was instrumental in the hand of God in saving Ulster from a veritable blood-bath.

There can be no doubting the genuineness of the vast majority of those converted in those days. Workers returned stolen property to their employers. People paid outstanding bills long overdue. At Harland and Wolff's shipyard it became necessary to erect a large shed to house the stolen property being returned. And these converts, in their hundreds, all across the Province, stood the test of time. There was nothing superficial in Nicholson's work, no "easy-believe-ism", no merely emotional response. Nicholson's emphasis on repentance was too sustained and his preaching of the Cross too powerful for that. As men and women listened to him they were stricken. This was the work of the Holy Spirit.

That something remarkable was taking place in the North of Ireland in those days was recognised by all. Under God, Nicholson had taken Ulster by storm and the place was shaken. The father of the present writer was passing through the town of Sligo in the early twenties and had occasion to call at a chemist's shop. No other customer was present. In the course of conversation it transpired that the chemist was an atheist. When Nicholson's work was mentioned, the chemist replied, "Nicholson is a British agent sent over by the authorities to calm things down!" Things certainly did calm down, but not because of any human agency.

Over the years, W.P. Nicholson conducted campaigns in many countries. On a return visit to Ireland in 1959 he sustained a heart attack en-route and was taken to hospital in Cork city. After an illness of two weeks he died on Thursday, 29th October, aged 83. The funeral took place in his home town of Bangor. His headstone in Clandeboye Cemetery bears the inscription:

In loving memory of

Rev. William Patteson Nicholson, John 3:30

beloved husband of F. Elizabeth Nicholson

Born 3rd April, 1876 - Born again 22nd May, 1899

Called Home 29th October, 1959

This fearless, fiery preacher could appeal to sinners to come to Christ in tones of tenderness and love. He as a man of prayer - daily he spent hours alone with God. Nicholson, with his rugged forthright preaching, touched the hearts of Belfast's shipyard workers as very few preachers could have done. He had gifts in evangelism that few possessed. Fearless, passionate, often controversial, he was the man for the moment - God's man. Who knows the outcome of *just one conversion*?

EPILOGUE

❖

Y ou have read the account of these twenty-eight conversions, which show what God does *in* the life of the one whose sins are forgiven, and what God does *through* that life to lead others to Himself. Two important questions need to be addressed.

Are you converted? In other words, have you in penitence and faith looked to Christ for salvation and put your trust completely in Him, acknowledging Him as your Saviour and King? You may be religious in a formal kind of way. You may give intellectual assent to the truths of Scripture. You may sincerely endeavour to live a respectable and moral life. Yet if you have not come to Christ with the burden of your sin, you have not found rest for your soul. Your righteousness falls short of God's requirement by an infinite distance. "All our righteousnesses are as filthy rags" in God's sight (Isa. 64:6).

Conversion, however, is not just a necessity for those who are steeped in what are considered the grosser sins. There is a widely held belief that if a person is kind and loving, compassionate and generous, he or she must go to Heaven. Multitudes hold this view and find it inconceivable that God would send such a person to hell. If this were true, there would have been no need for Christ to suffer and die on the cross in order to save sinners. Such thinking has no awareness of God's immaculate holiness, of His inflexible right-eousness, of the malignant and unclean nature of sin, or of the power of Satan in a fallen world. Only the power of God can deliver from the Evil One. Christianity is the only religion that proclaims salva-tion by grace *alone*, and salvation by a personal Saviour who ever lives and who may be known and loved. All other religions teach salvation in whole or in part by human endeavour. God's Word declares that salvation is "not by works of righteousness which we have done" (Titus 3:5).

This is not to overlook the fact that as Christians we are "created in Christ Jesus unto good works, which God hath before ordained that we should walk in them" (Eph. 2:10). We are not saved *by* works, neither are we saved *without* works - the new birth results in a new life. James, the brother of our Lord, writes, "Faith without works is dead" (2:26). In other words it is spurious and counterfeit. Evangelicals rightly reject the notion of salvation by works, so dear to the heart of fallen man, but they do need to avoid the opposite error of overlooking the vital place of good works in the Christian life - for without those works, saving faith is absent and the life remains unchanged. The men and women whose conversions are described in these pages showed their faith by their works, works motivated by love for God and done for His glory. Love for God ensures love for one's neighbour (Matt. 22:37-39). The unconverted often imagine that their own good works, seen as meritorious, will earn them a place in Heaven, but the Bible makes it plain that without faith it is impossible to please God (Heb. 11:6). Apart from Christ and His finished work there is no salvation.

The second question concerns the Christian. *Are you obedient in witnessing for your Saviour?* In this book you have read of men and women who were valiant for Christ and His truth. They were constrained by the love of Christ to work and witness for Him, often at great personal cost. They "hazarded their lives for the name of our Lord Jesus Christ" (Acts 15:26). While others talked, they obeyed. They could not but speak the things that they had seen and heard (Acts 4:20). They had heard Christ say, "go work *today* in my vineyard" (Matt. 21:28). Matthew Henry says, "God sets His children to work though they are all heirs. This command is given to every one of us". He adds, "We are not sent into the world to be idle, nor had we daylight given us to play by; and therefore, if ever we mean to do anything for God and our souls, why not now? Why not today?" Reader, what is your response to Christ's urgent call to work while it is day? "The night cometh when no man can work" (John 9:4).